The Teacher

POEMS AND OTHER WRITINGS

DUANE BROXSON

Order this book online at www.trafford.com
or email orders@trafford.com

Most Trafford titles are also available at major online book retailers.

Cover Design by Duane L.Broxson.
Photography by Duane L. Broxson.
The back cover is presented in memory of two special friends;
Dr. James Leonard Wolfe and Aviation Chief Mac Mckenny.

Printed in Victoria, BC, Canada.

ISBN: 978-1-4251-5525-4 (sc)
ISBN: 978-1-4251-7854-3

*Our mission is to efficiently provide the world's finest, most comprehensive
book publishing service, enabling every author to experience success.
To find out how to publish your book, your way, and have it available
worldwide, visit us online at www.trafford.com/*

Trafford rev. 1/8/10

 www.trafford.com

North America & international
toll-free: 1 888 232 4444 (USA & Canada)
phone: 250 383 6864 ♦ fax: 812 355 4082

Contents

Expositions 331

Preface

*R*eflections is a personal collection of writings accumulated over the years as I attempted to give expression to my emotions and feelings. My life has been a spiritual search. One conducted through the insights of Biblical Scripture, knowledge and deep introspection. I have felt a profound spiritual connection to almost everything I have confronted in the "natural" world.

This volume could have been called "My Struggle", although it was a healthy and wholesome struggle. It has been a struggle with the spiritual aspects of life. A struggle with science and religion not between them. I have always been fascinated with life, learning and knowledge. I have always embraced the principles of science in its objective search for knowledge and "truth".

As David Rosenburg, author of "Abraham" has said of others, my life experience is the stage upon which I have created my writings. If someone should read a line of mine and sense my emotion, feeling and meaning and be inspired to speak from the reaches of their own heart, I will have accomplished all I have desired.

The letters, particularly to Dr. Gould, represents part of a journey that is not yet over. One that began long before I knew of Natural History Magazine or Dr. Gould. Actually, it began in my early childhood as

I became acutely aware of the human condition. I remember as if it were yesterday, when this struggle to understand the nature of life began. I remember the first questions I asked myself as a very young child, riding up highway eighty seven north of Milton Florida in an old pick up truck with my dad. Why is life so fragile? Why will I eventually lose those loved ones to the inevitability of our situation on planet Earth? Why is this so and what is the meaning of it all? I loved my parents so much that I actually hoped I would die before they did because I could not bear the thought of losing either one of them. Of course, I was very young when those thoughts crossed my mind. Later on in life, I realized my death would be an even greater burden and loss to them.

I was reared as a Presbyterian Christian by my mother and her sister, but my father was not a member of the church. My dad though, seemed to live in the everyday of life according to the moral and ethical values I was being taught as a Christian. He was a very humble man though physically and mentally powerful and strong. His total commitment and love for all of his family, and my mothers unquestionable love for him, made me a family man. The behaviors I was taught in church I saw first hand in everyday experience in my mother and father.

As I studied Biblical Scripture, I became captivated by the spirituality and emotion found in the breathtakingly beautiful writings, especially Psalms and Isaiah. I read them over and over just to experience the powerful drama, and the emotion and spirituality they aroused in me, but I had a mind of my own. From the beginning I embraced the moral and ethical principles and teaching but questioned many of the underlying assumptions, what I recognize today as dogmatic fundamentalist doctrines. I was not one to just blindly embrace everything that people of religious conviction taught. Several leaders urged me to consider the ministry and I did consider this calling. I knew I had many unanswered questions that were not going to be answered by anyone but myself. The life and teaching of Jesus was a profound inspiration to me regardless of my questions. I always had a spiritual "connection" to the Suffering Servant and the visions of righteousness portrayed by the great prophets. I had powerful emotions and feeling. They came from the love I received throughout my childhood. Though loving, my people were not weak people. They were tough and strong mentally and physically, pioneers in a rough and rugged land. My immediate family possessed no real racial prejudice which was remarkable considering the area and time in which we lived. The women were virtuous and the men were men of character and principle. We cared for each other and respected each other deeply. I knew from the beginning I had been blessed to have been a part of these great families. Their life and values resonating with the teachings of the Bible left me with a sincere yearning for righteousness and a deep feeling of spirituality. I knew I could love. I had been loved. I had a genuine empathy for others. I knew I could care. I had been cared for. I wanted so much to give back what I had received, to be a positive influence in the world for "good". I felt I could become a dynamic preacher, but my questions and my spiritual "honesty" would not allow me to do this.

I decided I would find out all I could about the natural world. I would study science. I would learn to fly. I loved aviation. I entered Junior College at Pensacola Florida and received some of the best liberal arts instruction available in the nation at the time. I later transferred to a small college in Alabama where I continued my study of science, graduating with a bachelor's degree in Medical Technology.

My motive was to learn. I had a thirst for knowledge and embraced completely the objective techniques and principles of science. I knew when I studied geology, paleontology and biology that some of those doubts I had about fundamental doctrine were real and had a basis in truth. I knew for sure when I studied Romer's comparative anatomy that evolutionary biology was a powerful and profound objective truth about the living world around me. I was not frightened by this revelation. I expected it. I had long questioned the "creation stories" found in the earliest Biblical Scriptures and knew that the details lay elsewhere. Still, I had a genuine love for the Biblical Scriptures and for their writers, and knew they were inspired to write with their own hand, with their own minds great visions of righteousness which had profound influence on mankind for "good".

As I pursued my various careers in science, first as a Medical Technologist in a hospital laboratory and later as a teacher of science, I read and studied all I could understand about science and enjoyed every minute of it. The new insights and knowledge stirred my imagination. I was no less enthused about my newly discovered evolving world than I had been perplexed over the created world of my previous doubts, yet my spirituality was still powerful and strong. I still felt a spiritual connection to the dynamic teachings of the Bible.

Science was not the only material I read. With the mind of an objective realist and the heart of a spiritual mystic, I read all about religion and religions that I could. This included several volumes about the history of the Christian Church and Christianity. I was appalled and dumbfounded at the inhumanity of some of Christian mankind. I would not read what I thought were biased commentaries written by theologians. I read the secular scholars of Hebrew writing and literature, the archeological finds by objective scientists. I journeyed into the world of Eastern Religions and some of the commentaries written about them. I read all of the Gnostic writings and some of the commentaries written about them. All of this only made my vision clearer and my need stronger to embrace and understand that spiritual essence of nature that had produced Abrahams, Isaacs, Jacobs, Davids, Isaiahs, Buddahas, Ramakirshnas, Mohammads, and the Jesus of my own Christian heritage.

All of this activity was possible because it blended naturally with my profession of thirty five years, that of a teacher of science in the secondary high school. Because of the small school in which I taught, I was responsible for all of the science there for many years. I taught seventh, eighth and ninth grade science, physics, chemistry, biology, environmental science, earth science and astronomy as well as classes of advanced mathematics at various times. As I studied and taught these disciplines and read the writings of religious nature I mentioned, I became convinced that the fundamentalist preachers of the Bible Belt and Christianity in general needed desperately to embrace new enlightenments. To me, they were literally teaching things a nominally educated person in the twentieth century could understand to be false. To me, they needed to study with the intent to learn, the evolutionary biology of the twentieth century. They needed to read Bart D. Erhman's "Misquoting Jesus", and of course, Timothy Paul Jones's "Misquoting Truth". They needed to quit reading the Pentateuch with blind eyes, and read "David and Solomon" by Israel Finkelstein and Neil Asher Silberman. They needed to realize they may be teaching the words of a woman writer when they try to pound home their dogmatic doctrines of the Genesis by reading David Rosenberg's "Abraham". Does this mean they need to abandon the great moral and ethical teachings of Jesus and the Old Testament? Obviously not. They need to realize (in my opinion) the Biblical writings are an evolution in themselves, the evolution of human vision and righteousness. The inspiration (devine or otherwise) coming from within themselves as they struggled with the experiences of life. I have not forsaken the Jesus of their teaching, just some of *their* teaching that I can know and understand with the knowledge of the twenty first century to be false. I have only embraced him more fully with a broader perspective and an open mind.

I began to believe after many years that this "God" we seek is not out "there" somewhere, but is present within the essence of our own being and within the fabric of our own observable universe, that the natural aspects of ourselves and nature contained the spiritual essence. It's best human expression, being agape love. Some of the writings about Jesus emphasize this thought. Even in the standard orthodox canonized writings about Jesus one can find this insight. According to the writings, once Jesus was speaking with the teachers of the law and instructed them not to look here or there for the kingdom because the kingdom was within them. And of course, the beautiful teachings of the orthodox Gospel of John and the Epistles of John indicating that you cannot love (that is in my opinion to know) God and hate your brother and the outright concept that "God" is love. I remember in my heart and soul today the teachings in song of my earliest childhood. "Praise Him, Praise Him, all you little children. God is love, God is love." What a beautiful teaching! What a beautiful concept! Love is a real thing, a real experience that has a very human expression in the *now*. An expression that brings man close to the *spiritual* essence of human nature, and of "God".

I began to read Natural History Magazine after subscribing sometime prior to nineteen hundred eighty three. I became interested in a standing article, "This View of Life", written by Stephen Jay Gould. At first I had to read parts of his article several times in order to understand all of his thoughts and metaphorical bridges. I had to consult my dictionary. I knew right away he was no ordinary writer. I learned he was a Harvard Professor, was Jewish and also an a-theist. His writings on evolutionary principles were educating and fascinating. I began to see into his genuine concern for humanity and his knowledge of Biblical Scripture. I became aware of his objection to creationism and intelligent design as a part of a science educational program or curriculum, or as part of science at all for that matter.

I had been reading many articles in scientific journals and magazines and was up to date on the latest insights of science in most of the disciplines. This was particularly true concerning the evolutionary aspects of modern biological research. Quantum physics was also fascinating with its newly found metaphysical ramifications. I attended scientific institutes and in-service training sponsored by the local university and taught by its faculty. I began to see a connection between the metaphysical aspects of quantum mechanics , the great physicists search for "truth" about our universe and our own spiritual search for the essence we called "God". I could see clearly that we "are" what we are trying to understand and explain in the physical world of physics. It was not two systems, the observing system and the observed system. It was one system observing itself. Also, to me, man's consciousness was a natural player in the evolution of life on earth and all of man's activities were part of the only nature we know. This thought radiated from reflections upon the very essence of reality and not from a trivial play on words as to what is natural. Day after day in the scientific journals I could see scientists, I thought, doing what they had so harshly criticized the earliest thinkers of doing. That is, viewing man as a kind of supernatural influence on the "natural" nature that we knew and studied and that his intent and will were destroying "natural nature" as if his will and culture existed apart form the "natural world" they were so intently studying. Also, science and religion, I thought, desperately needed to be interfaced by the creative aspects of humankind in the twentieth century. We needed new religious enlightenment, powered by the new insights of modern scientific research. We needed to build upon the spiritual insights of thousands of years of human experience in the light of our own new knowledge and clearer understanding. Grave problems and pressing demands almost dictated this for the survival of modern human civilization. No trivial matter in my way of thinking.

That is why I responded to Dr Gould's article "The Most Unkindest Cut of All" that appeared in This View of Life in Natural History Magazine, May, of nineteen hundred ninety two. Even though I agreed with Dr. Gould concerning the use of scientific principles to justify one's evil deeds, I felt Hitler was using a scientific insight about the functioning of the natural world to accomplish his goals. He really was influencing the unfolding of natural history by his actions. I challenged Dr. Gould's view of what is natural. What ensued spanned many years continuing until "This View of Life" retired from the pages of Natural History Magazine and Dr. Gould, very sadly so, went "by way of all the earth".

I hope you will read these letters. To understand their full meaning and connection to the writings of Dr. Gould, one would need to correlate and read the articles of "This View of Life" that motivated my responses. The letters were not written to be published. They are not scientific papers and were not written to be considered as such. They were deliberately written with a mix of science, philosophy, religion and personal reflections. We had a conversation together about life, about science and evolution, and about religion, through the pages of Natural History Magazine. It was a great journey for me, motivating and stimulating my personal creative activity and making me glad and proud to have been a small and unseen part of "This View of Life".

Reflections

Light of All Lights

As the light that stems from a light house in the height of a storm guides those in peril away from danger, so it is with the love of God toward all men. It is an ever guiding and directing light that gives men faith to travel on even when the end is not sure.

Oh light of all lights! Shine forth thy beauty to all the worlds. Glow with an ever increasing warmth. Harken not at the dismal turmoil of space, falter not at the pit of nothingness, but shine on through all eternity, never fading, never more beginning or ceasing. Glow with a radiance of good, shine with a ray of hope, enlighten thy path with the strong bond of faith, and live for ever as a humble heart in the minds of men.

Let it be the ruler of all good, the donor of all truth, the essence of all faithfulness, and the regulator of all power. Let it be aggressive yet kind, straightforward yet humble, powerful yet meek. Let it shine forth in all its' splendor in the hearts of men, ever binding, ever being, ever holding, ever lasting. Never to falter lest all men fall. Never to fail lest all men die.

My Struggle

Once beneath the bonds of time and fear,
I struggled with the might of all the world,
A might which, like the spear will pierce the heart,
Will pierce the soul and send you searching in all your sorrow
The happiness you once spent.

Yet above these bonds I rose,
all conquering fear and time,
I found the joy of life,
In the heart of the loving kind.

And in this love I'll tread
The pathways of my life,
Till my last prayer is said,
And God takes up my fight.

Two Views of Life

Lights sights jackets crowds,
In the wang dang of life.
Popping bottles mixing like
A system of confusion.

Hang the mark! Let it ride!
Ding flop rattle chattle.
Everest's mount a cactus kittle,
In the wang dang of life.

Hights rights goals loves,
In the wang dang of life.
Sing fling upsoar!
Simple straightfull might!

Live the song the striving life
Ever forward morrow.
Everest's mount a graceful soaring
In the wang dang of life!

In Memory of Gay

I stand alone in the breeze that blows
So gently through the trees,
That flows o'er mountains high,
And across the bounding seas.

I face the gentle flow of air
As it crosses o'er the way,
And that you someday it may reach,
To God I softly pray.

I know that I could never gain
The place where you now stand,
But I can send the gentle breeze
That blows across the land.

I can send the gentle breeze
That blows, that blows away,
My memory of a past time spent,
And prayer for a brighter day.

DUANE BROXSON. THE TEACHER

On Love

To lose one's love
Is to lose one's life,
For to love is to live,
To live is to learn to know love.

To love is to know God,
To hate is to know no love.
To not know love or to lose it,
Is to know hell or find it!

Losing One's Love

Her golden hair a-flowing,
The star light in her eyes a-glowing
The voice of her warm heart singing,
Made me to love her.

Her golden hair a-flowing,
The starlight in her eyes a-glowing,
The voice of her warm heart singing,
Made me to lose her.

When love is come and then is gone,
Sweet somber sorrow
Melts all feeling of long loved laughter.

Love's Heartbreak

Ah Love,
Is it joy? Is it laughter?
Is it part of God's hereafter?
She was beautiful and fair
With loving eyes and flowing hair,
Like the sparkling rays of morning,
Like the brilliance of the day,
Like the gentle beams of twilight
Painting colors on the bay!

Ah Love,
What's the price one has to pay
Just to give his heart away?
The price I paid was pain and sorrow,
Shattered hopes of life's tomorrow.
Like the cold and wintery morning,
Like the cloudy darkened day,
Like the chilly breezes blowing
On a cold and lonely bay.

"Oh, but could I give my heart away again,
I would."

From Whence We Came

Oh mighty hills!
Straining beneath the burning noonday sun.
I see your majestic timber painting colors beneath the
cloud blotched breathless blue sky,
And watch your shadows play across the sparkling
springs that caress your gentle valleys and fall from
rocky cliffs to mirrored pools of shaded blue below.

Oh mighty hills!
Beneath whose rolling timber lie the timeless trails and
hidden footprints of man from distant ages, who also
looked in awe and wondered why and what and where
and when.

Oh mighty hills!
Holder of the secrets of man's past hidden age.
I've seen your mighty heights worn down and cast and
carried tumbling toward the sea, to make a record in
another place of future pasts in the timeless trails of
man.

Oh mighty hills!
From whence we came, fashioned from the essence
of your weathered mass to grasp you in our hand and
from you form the many splendors of our time.

DUANE BROXSON. THE TEACHER

Oh mighty hills!
From within whose waters you enclose we came to
cast our spirits from the darkness of your caves into
the light of brilliant day and fashion from you the
images of our reckoned selves.

Oh mighty hills!
From the distant reaches of the Universe we came,
fired and formed from the gaseous nebula of a fusing
star and flung through endless space among a billion
unnamed stars. With you we rode, unknown and
unformed through the distant ages of the past to be
thrown upon this age and hurtled onward.

Oh mighty hills!
"I will both lay me down in peace and sleep", "I will
both lay me down in peace and sleep", beneath these
hills, beneath these hills from whence I came. "I will
both lay me down in peace and sleep", and await the
dawning of another age.

To The Physicists

Up quark, down quark
All around are strange quarks.
Charm quark, beauty quark,
Maybe there's a truth quark!

This track, that track
Physicists their minds rack.
This way, that way,
They turned into a gamma ray!

This mark, that mark,
All this is in a meadow lark?!
This for certain, that for certain,
Yet in the end it's uncertain.

This law, that law,
And we do get bolder,
This truth, that truth,
Maybe the beholder?

DUANE BROXSON. THE TEACHER

I The Watcher

I see the light sea breezes blowing the sparkling splashing spray.

I feel the mighty surge of the ocean's awesome waves and hear them pound upon the shore's defenseless rock

I taste the ocean's salty air and lift my somber spirit to the sky and watch the gulls sail the flowing waves of ocean air.

Sail for a while and then be done. Wonder for a while and then be done.

And I the watcher through the countless moments of future time am watched by eyes unknown and spirits yet unborn.

Why and Where and When

Across the mighty boundless rolling seas,
And rising neath the dimly lighted arc of earth,
Spreading sparkling spangle of orange and red across
the greyish sky,
The mighty restless surging sun sprays out upon
the earth her magic rays,
That bathes the forest glens and hills and filters down
among the many colored trees.

And yet a million, billion, burning suns of glittering,
gleaming, glowing, glare,
Appear from pole to pole and mark this place upon a depthless
Charted window of celestial sphere.

As one before, I ponder why and where and when.
I look upon it all but see it from within.
I try to capture it with rhyme,
I am a moment of a place in space and time.

DUANE BROXSON. THE TEACHER

To Jerry Hunter

Out of the searing, surging storms of a nuclear inferno,
Flung across an eternity of galactic time,
Coalescing from the spent remains of a burned out star,
I am.

Red Giant, White Dwarf, Supernova,
All a part of the Great Jehovah?
Twinkle, twinkle awesome star,
I am a part of what you are!

Joys of Life

A sandy summer road with little pebbles lying there,

A breeze that moves about through forest trees,
That sways the towering pine and russells to and
fro the many colored leaves.

A brook whose crystal water mingles with the torrents of a
thousand other streams.

A soaring cloud silhouetted against a sunlit sky of blue.

A star filled night that spreads from pole to pole,
A billion twinkles from a distant place in time.

A hope, a care, a touch, a smile,
A life that's filled with love.

Suffer the Little Children

I lifted up my soul and cried aloud through the reaches
of the universe! I wandered a moment within a cloudy
nebula, then passed along to distant groups of stars.
I contemplated the awesome power of quasaar and
approached the outer limits of black holes. I saw a
twinkling light in the darkness of a dismal space, a
little flicker from the blackened space of man. And
then, a majestic force moved through the eternity of
the universe! Its light was like the purity of generations
of humble people and loving friends. It sent its beams
to an anguished earth and danced upon the hearts of
little children, and from them, here and there, pierced
the selfish soul of man. Their little hearts so pure and
full of love! Oh linger in the hearts of little children,
and wipe the darkness from the face of man!

Reach Out Oh Soul of Freedom

My soul is free!
Free as the mighty wind that blows among the trees,
Among the bending boughs and falling autumn leaves,
And falling autumn leaves of brown and gold and grey.

Soar oh wind!
Above the majestic heights of earth's own land,
And down, down, down among the timeless trails of man,
And feel the earth its' mighty forces move,
And with a touch, a gentle breeze,
Reach out! Reach out!

DUANE BROXSON. THE TEACHER

The Joy of Life

Love has passed all hate and fear,
Gone are the evils of long passed time,
Through the town ring songs of praise,
And in the night the church bells chime.

Man has found the joy of life,
Not in the gift but the giver,
A fulfilling joy that moves the heart
And dwells with man forever.

For in this love of God and Man,
Dwell all the truth of this great earth,
All the power of life Devine,
And all the things of worth.

To Cindy

And the students said:
"Tell us Teacher, what is a sunrise?"
And the Teacher said:
"A sunrise is a dawning, a promise for the unfolding day."
And the students said:
"Tell us, tell us about the sunshine."
And the Teacher said:
"The sunshine is a radiance, a life giving force that energizes
our day."
And the students said:
"And what about sunsets? Do you know about sunsets?"
And the Teacher replied:
"Yes, A sunset is a hope, a longing, waiting for another dawn."
Then a young and sensitive student said:
"What about friendships? Do you know about friendships?"
And the Teacher replied:
"Yes, I know about friendships. A friendship is a dawning,
a dawning of radiant sunshine, a life giving force that adds
purpose to our day."
And another student said:
"Do friendships have sunsets?"
And the Teacher said:
"Yes, but sunsets bring memories, and hopes, and a longing for
another dawn."

DUANE BROXSON. THE TEACHER

With Love for Daniel

When I consider how he came and met
The many rigid requirements set,
And how with sparkle in his eyes
He hustled hard to get his prize,
Although he knew right from the start,
He'd be denied a meaningful part,
And when his work fell on deaf ear,
Mid praise of others he could hear,
He hustled hard to please his dad,
Even though within his heart was sad.
And as I watched and wondered why,
I did not offer a reply,
For deep within this gentle heart,
Lives a home run hitter for God's park.

To Mother

When I think on thee,
I think on one I love so much.
I'm reminded of the roses of the valley,
The ones I like to touch.
How beautiful those blossoms are,
As is your life to me.
Fragrant in the valley they bloom
And send their air a-far,
So I in all my life your love will be,
Through all the world, my cares, my aims, my heart, my life,
my all,
Will think on thee,
Will think on thee in happy memory,
The one I love so much.

To Dad

When I think of all that's good,
That's honest and is true,
I know I'll never find
A fellow quite like you.

So friendly and so kind
To every one around,
A sort of shining light,
Among the men of town.

You labor and you toil,
From day until the night,
And rest with peace abiding,
Beneath the soft lamp light.

You never want to quarrel
Or fight to gain the world,
You have a love of life,
More precious than a pearl.

You're one who loves our Nation,
Who loves our sacred land,
A humble hearted person,
A good and honest man.

So through the trials of life
Of one thing I am glad,
I knew a certain fellow,
And that fellow, was my dad.

The Launch of Saturn Five

Flint rock struck flint rock
And the spark of fire it raised,
Among the kindling shavings
Formed man's first fiery blaze.

The rocket slowly lifted skyward,
With a mighty blast of flame,
Ever slowly rising upward,
O'er the hills and rocks and plains.

Onward men!

I Am

I've seen the snow capped mountains high
And heard the rumbling river's roar.
I've felt the heat of burning fire
And touched the placid waters cool.

I am my failing eyes and ageing face,
I am my joy and tender caring.
I am my fumbling hands and stumbling feet,
I am my hope and future vision.

I am the battered driftwood of a thousand storm wrecked ships,
I am the memory of a thousand battles won.
I am the rageing fire of every tyrant's sword,
I am the pleasant peace of all men's spirits gentle.

I am the subtle star light of every one I've known,
I am myself the burning noon day sun,
Here and now is what I am,
Now and when is what I will be.
I am a moment of a place in space and time,
I rest among a billion unnamed stars.

The Work of God

I've seen the valleys lying silent in the forest,
I've seen the hills rise up and send their towering timber to meet the
sky.
I've seen the creeks and swamps and lakes and rivers,
I've seen the deer go slipping by.

I've seen the bud that made the flower,
The child that made the man,
I've seen the storm and summer shower,
The rock, the sea, the sand.

And often times when looking back
On trails some men have trod,
I stop and think, and then I know,
I've seen the work of God.

Faith and Doubt

All things made? All things are?
Things good, Things bad,
Time space, space time,
An infinity, an eternity.

Eternity, infinity far away time,
Granite rock of the Faith,
Drifting sand of the doubt.

Rock, sand, doubt, faith.
All things are? All things made?

A Little Child

Behold the beauty of a little child!
Its heart pours forth all the splendor of a loving God,
And its smile is like the radiance of the loving Christ!

Tears

The tears they flow,
They glisten in the light,
Tears of joy to know one's love
Yet know one's plight.

Her eyes they meet with mine,
They sparkle,
They are so loving kind.

To Jerrie

When in those special moments I meet you,
I see the beauty of a pretty smile,
And from your glowing radiant face
Your sparkling eyes reach out
And greet with warm embrace.

And in that moment,
In the twinkling starlight of your eyes,
I see the springtime of earth pass by
With all the fragrance of its woodland flowers in full bloom.
For as the mystic magic of your eyes meet mine,
I feel the power of our Earth's eternal spring,
Flowing like a fountain from within, unseen.

I see the towering timber on the rolling hills of Earth,
And walk beneath the boughs of brown and gold and green,
I hear the whispering wind from the mountain peaks come down,
And watch the lofty eagle soar among the clouds.
And from the depths of Earth, I feel a moving spirit flow,
And watch the Earth unfold in scenes of wondrous joy.

And if, perchance, someday my dreams come true,
It's sure that all the earth would only bloom to me
In flowers of spring!

DUANE BROXSON. THE TEACHER

A Sad Day's Journey
(Manistee)

O'er the hills, and down the meadows,
From the mountains to the sea.
I feel a yearning calling,
And its memory beckons me.

It fills my mind with feeling,
That memory by the sea,
It fills my mind with feeling,
For I stop and think on thee.

In the pines, in the pines,
Your memory lingers near the pines,
On the hill side by the mill site,
Near that valley of the pines.

Though your voice be steady calling,
From my heart felt need for the,
Though my life be filled with yearning,
I will never be with thee.

All I have is fleeting memories
In my soul a-thirst for thee,
All I have is fleeting memories,
For I'll never be with thee.

Though my soul be strongly yearning,
Though my life be full and free,
It will be a sad day's journey,
From the hills of Manistee'.

Reflections

Caring is Forever

The seas fill up and evaporate into the sky.
The ice spreads in continental sheets and melts away.
The mountains rise up and are worn down.
Civilizations rise to power and are trampled in destruction.
The machines of man wither to rubble and dust.
All of the magnificent mansions of man return to the elements from
which they came.
The finest finished steel atomizes in the heated conflagration of the
Red Giant..
Nothing on this earth is forever.

The love of a mother and father grows with tender caring.
The young one's heart leaps with joy and sings the song of his fam-
ily's love.
The love of a mother and father grows with tender caring.
The young one's heart leaps with joy and sings the song of his fam-
ily's love.
The love of a mother and father grows with tender caring.
The young one's heart leaps with joy and sings the song of his fam-
ily's love.
Through the generations, their souls sing their silent song and freely
give their tender caring.
The Red Giant sears all memory from the face of the living Earth.
The spirits of the caring souls have returned to the superstate from
which they emanated.
Caring is forever.

DUANE BROXSON. THE TEACHER

The Love of David and Janine

The pleasures of this Earth I can find,
Its wine and its women can be mine
But to have them I know I must trade,
The love of my Neanie and my Dave,

It was there I met their mother in the beauty of the night,
And I learned to love her, our children my delight,
But she turned and left me, our children she did trade,
The hurt, oh the hurt, will be mine in my grave.

Hi hi hee, Where is my little boy?
Hi hi hee, Where is my little girl?
Gone gone away, Gone gone away,
So far away from me.

What's missing in this old earthly place?
What's missing in this old selfish world?
Well, it's love for the little Davie boys,
And it's love for the little Neanie girls.

The glitter of the night clubs and the sound of the band,
The pleasures and the sins of this lush, plush land,
Traded for the love of my Neanie and my Dave,
The hurt, oh the hurt, will be mine in my grave

Hi hi hee, Where is my little boy?
Hi hi hee, Where is my little girl?
Gone , gone away, Gone, gone away,
So far away from me.

I cannot change this old earthly place,
I cannot change this old selfish world,
But I can hug my little Davie boy,
And I can kiss my little Neanie girl.

The beauty of their mother was as roses in the breeze,
But beneath the roses was the tempest of the seas,
Rushing, crushing, dashing, its torrent to the shore,
The hurt, oh the hurt, will be mine evermore.

Hi hi hee, Where is my little boy?
Hi hi hee, where is my little girl?
Gone, gone away, Gone, gone away,
So far away from me.

Almost There[1]

Almost there, almost there,
Just one kiss,
We were almost there.

Almost there, almost there,
From one missed kiss,
A heartbreak's despair.

Almost there, almost there,
Would you know
The pain I'd bear?

Almost there, almost there,
A life together shattered,
But I'll always care.

I heard a preacher,
From the pulpit swear,
He's missed his heaven,
And Its hell to bear.

Don't worry mister preacher,
Because I'm already there,
For it's all about caring,
Not some place up there.

A place can only shatter,
And come to an end,
But caring is forever,
It's a spirit from within.

---

[1] This writing concers experiences prior to 1985.

To University Hospital

Oh University!
Why have you gone, Oh University?
Champion of those who lived in adversity.
Not garnished with riches or societal frills,
Not teeming with surgeons with unheard of skills,
Not blessed with outrageous insurance paid bills,
But filled with a heart to serve helpless mens' ills.

Oh University!
You will be missed , Oh University!
But most by those who lived in adversity.

I was a part time employee in the laboratory at University Hospital for many years. I had grown to be proud I worked there. There were so many helpless and ill people who were being served there. I remember once being asked about my part time hospital work by a rather affluent person. I said, "I work at University Hospital." Somewhat deflated, the person had said "Oh." As if to work there was rather mundane. How I knew different! The laboratory had some of the most professional and well trained personnel in Pensacola. Many of the nurses were real servants with great ability. Numerous professionals gave of their expertise and experience to the helpless people who came there. Many doctors received some of their training there where their knowledge and skill had to be applied under some of the most difficult circumstances. Many great things are often overlooked in society because of our priorities and perspectives. Great things were accomplished by University Hospital regardless of its financial struggle. It was a privilege to have worked there.

Much of this work has been continued by Sacred Heart Hospital where, there again, the great service becomes embedded and obscured in the financial difficulty of modern medicine. The work is done nevertheless and people's lives are mended and given hope. A hand is held out. A Sacred Heart, as always, is offered to the people.

From Father to Son

Father:

"Above all things get knowledge and understanding"

Son:

"Do I get knowledge and understanding to please you father?"

Father:

"No, you get knowledge and understanding so that you can find your place in your world in your time and love your son in his time."

Son:

"Will my knowledge and understanding be your knowledge and understanding?"

Father:

"No son, for my time is just the beginning of your time as my life was just the beginning of your life."

Son:

"All life flows from other life and all knowledge and understanding flows with it through the countless ages?"

Father:

"Yes. I am both old and new, both new and old."

Son:

"How is this so my beloved father?"

Father:

"I am old for I have flowed from my ancient ancestors carrying with me the life force that sustains us. I am new because I am a new expression in a new age."

Son:

"Oh my father, will I see through both visions in my search for knowledge and understanding?"

Father:

"Yes my son, but you must never let the visions of the past obscure the visions of the future, for you live not in past time but at the threshold of the door of future time. You must look through the door, my son, so when your son takes your place, he too may desire to look through."

Son:

"Oh my father, if you could only go with me and share my visions in my time!"

Father:

"I will be there my son, for we are bound by the continuous outpouring of our souls. I will be there as a whisper, a guide, a memory. I will be the threshold upon which you stand and look. Look! Look! Look now, for my door is closing."

Reflections

Your Love is Our Hope[2]

Oh happy, laughing, loved brothers in the home,
Would I with all your joy your knowledge share,
But I'm denied by nature, "red in tooth and claw",
I must within an extra burden bear.

But yet somehow with chance still comes a joy,
With love and hope and caring all around,
For yet with scar, I'm blessed with greater hope,
A home where grace and love abound.

So as this trek of life unfolds,
Within the souls of man,
Seeing with our minds and hearts,
Enacting with our hands,

We'll strive with all to take a stand,
A grand dimension new,
And with our wills we'll melt the law,
That makes us "red in tooth and claw".

---

[2] This was written when I observed the love of a family for its down's syndrome member. A love that was open, and enjoined him with others. A love that was unashamed and caring. God bless this family.

DUANE BROXSON. THE TEACHER

The Insight of the Masses, Bless Their Hearts

PREACHER:
Anyone with any common sense should know that the
Earth is really flat. Why, these pseudo-intellectuals, all
caught up in their evolutionary theories and equations
are just corrupting the minds of our children. We
should just burn the universities, if that's all they can
come up with, and send these fellows off to the funny
farm where they belong.

THE MASSES:
And all the people said, "Amen!"

BUT THE TEACHER SAID
    TO THE PREACHER:
Come now and listen with open ears ready to hear,
it really is spherical. Look! Look! We can tell by the
light and the shadow in the well. We can tell by the
shadow that it casts. The power of our inward spirit
has allowed us to observe and discern this. The Holy
Father of our life spirit has moved within us. We have
gained insight and we have seen and interpreted our
visions and they are real! Look! Look! See! Look now!

AND THE PREACHER SAID:
Where is your authority that you speak of the spirit.
Your spirit is not our spirit!

AND THE TEACHER SAID:
But our spirits condemn murders, adulteries,
fornications, thefts, and blasphemies and we have
strived so hard with all of the spirit that dwells within
us to be true witnesses of the visions we have seen.
The flat earth withers like the plant that dries up for
lack of water and is up-rooted and blown by the wind,
but the spherical earth blossoms forth with all the
beauty of its life ever changing upon it like the tree
planted by the rivers of water that cannot be moved!
Come let us reason together and plot a course that will
not fail for the people of our hearts!

AND THE PREACHER SAID:
We question not like your spirits and we look not to
the right or to the left so that our foot will not stumble,
that our path will be straight like our ancestors who
walked before us.

AND THE TEACHER SAID:
We too look with the eyes of our fathers and we see
also with the eyes of your fathers. Our struggle has
been to find the right path to knowledge just as your
struggle has been to reveal a right path to walk. The
spirit of the Holy Father does not condemn itself
within us and our path is also your path. We are all
called to a new dimension and a new time by the
constant unfolding of our world around us. From the
hearts and souls of our ancient fathers we are calling

you to embrace a new law, a new enlightenment. We have been flung forward by the hopes and visions of our fathers and have been guided by the hopes and visions of your fathers. As soul flows to soul we have gained insight.

AND THE PREACHER SAID:
One cannot gain insight lest it come from above.

AND THE TEACHER SAID:
We are wrestling in a sea of universe in which every direction is above. Have we been talking about anything less? The power and forces of our universe touch us from without but the power of our visions flow from the depths of our inner souls as we grope with our senses and find ourselves and plot our course in this universe! Oh universe! Do you see yourself through us? You are the essence of our heartbeat!

AND THE PREACHER SAID:
You walk a lonely path and few are here to comfort you!

AND THE TEACHER SAID:
Yes! Yes! A new insight is a lonely insight. At the moment of its inception it bursts forth from the yearnings and visions of our forefathers in glowing splendor and floods the essence of ourselves with profound revelation but turns and shakes the foundations upon which our fathers stood and makes null much of our tradition. And tradition dies hard. But the power of a vision of a new truth flows slowly forth from the insight of its few, from soul to struggling soul, until its profound power ferments within the

masses. And then with time, much time, it too becomes a tradition to be revisited.

AND THE PREACHER SAID:
You speak as though some of you should bear rejection and loneliness in your time for insight that destroys your tradition. How can we join hands with you in our time if it destroys the tradition that we preach?

AND THE TEACHER SAID:
You must carry forth the cross of a new enlightenment.

AND THE PREACHER ASKED:
The cross of a new enlightenment?

AND THE TEACHER SAID:
Yes. In the face of the tradition of men, He carried the cross of a new enlightenment.

AND THE MASTERFUL SERVANT SAID:
Amen.

Looking from My Classroom

Balmy Breezes Blew Beneath the Billowing Beacons of the Blue.
Behold! I am.

Balmy Breezes Blow Beneath the Billowing Beacons of the Blue.
I am?

Balmy Breezes Blow Beneath the Billowing Beacons of the Blue.

"This law that law and we do get bolder,
This truth that truth, maybe the beholder?"

Balmy Breezes Blow Beneath the Billowing Beacons of the Blue.

"I am a moment of a place in space and time."

Balmy Breezes Blow Beneath the Billowing Beacons of the Blue.

"We are a moment of a place in space and time."

Balmy Breezes Blow Beneath the Billowing Beacons of the Blue.
"Who sent you?" "I Am that I Am sent you."

Shimmering Streams of Surging Sun Streaks Across the Silent Slumbering Souls.

Behold! I am.
Who sent you?
I Am that I Am sent you..

Reflections

Little Brave Bent Feather

Little Brave Bent Feather:
Oh great Chief Light From the Sky, why do all braves
pray to the Spirit of our Gods for the Spirit the deer he
has just slain?

Great Chief Light From the Sky:
My strong brave Bent Feather, all life draws life from
other life. We pray for the Spirit of the deer because he
has given up his life to sustain our life. We know that
one day our own life will be called up to sustain other
life, for this is the way of our great forest. So we pray
for the spirit of the deer knowing that in our time the
great forest will find honor and purpose in our own
death.

Little Brave Bent Feather:
Oh Great Chief, knower of the Spirit of life, I will pray
for the spirit of the deer, that my Spirit might also be
lifted up by the great giver of life, the Spirit of the
Forest.

Great Chief Light From the Sky:
And when all life be lifted up, we will know the
knower and the brave and the deer will be one in the
spirit as they are one in the great forest which was
lifted up from the bowels of the bare earth.

The Heart of a Scale

Through the days of very hard planning,
Over the whole of six weeks spanning,
I have purposed the probable banning,
Of your scale.

But yet in rightful reason reckoning,
I feel within a conscience beckoning,
They're working, searching, driving, striving,
Don't end the scale.

So Ryan, Jason, Margaret, Sherman,
I have within my heart determined,
You've really truly been a learning!
I decree: The scale!

'Tis The Raven Nothing More

Far off in the woodland standing,
I think I see a raven landing,
Yes! Upon man's buildings standing,
Picking at a piece of worthless rubble
from the floor.
Standing, Picking at the floor,
Picking picking,
Picking at the floor,
Only this and nothing more.

As the bird began to plunder
It set my heart afire with wonder,
I wondered at man's world o'er which he soared.
O'er the banging clanging bustle,
O'er the madness of the hustle,
O'er the paved street concrete puzzle,
To spy a morsel for his picking,
A morsel for his picking,
Only this and nothing more?

Surely here he felt a yearning,
A moving need for its discerning,
To turn his mind away from plunder,
From picking at the plunder

From picking at the worthless plunder,
Picking picking,
Picking at the plunder,
Picking at the worthless plunder,
Only this and nothing more.

Only this and nothing more?
Did not all he see down under,
Set his heart afire with wonder,
Turn his thoughts away from picking,
Picking, picking
From picking at the plunder
Picking picking,
Picking for a morsel from the plunder,
Picking picking,
Only this and nothing more?

From the monoxide smelted railing,
To the hydrated hardened paving,
Peered the sharp eyed ruffled raven
For a morsel of his craving,
Craving craving,
For a morsel of his craving,
Only this and nothing more.

For a morsel of his craving?
What has set all nature raving
Save a morsel for its craving?
Craving craving,

A morsel for its craving,
Picking picking,
For its spirit inside raging,
Picking picking,
Picking for its craving,
Only this and nothing more.

Some in grander nobler measure,
Seek to satisfy their pleasure,
For a bust of Pallas yearning,
For a hope of life discerning,
From the pain of evil turning,
Let me open up a door!
That black bird bosom bore,
All the truth of quantum lore!
What a supernatural door!
Nay, 'tis just the raven nothing more!

I see him over yonder,
Picking for his plunder
Picking for his craving,
Craving craving,
Picking picking
Picking for his craving,
Picking through the worthless plunder
Picking with his heart I wonder?
Picking picking, picking picking,
Only this and nothing more?
Quote the raven, "Evermore!"

DUANE BROXSON. THE TEACHER

How Reckoned Are Deeds?

How reckoned are deeds,
In this land we do trod?
What some see as blasphemous,
Others as God.

We form what we think,
By how it is viewed,
Both in offering it up,
And as it's construed.

Some swear by Sir Darwin,
A truth there achieved,
But some that love Jesus,
Refuse to believe.

Some see in loved Jesus,
A beautiful seed,
While also in Darwin,
A masterful deed.

In search of sweet truth,
Take your hats off please,
For those that would reckon,
The fruits of both deeds.

And what could I offer,
For lives so sublime?
Only one looked forward,
One backward in time.

For Students at Christmas

What real gift could I give you at Christmas?

I would give you riches, but riches are not mine to
give.
I would give you health, but health is from luck and
your own nurture.
I would give you knowledge, but only you can drink at
the fountain of knowledge.
I would give you ambition, but I can only be a kindling
flame.
I would give you faith, but faith comes only through
your own soul searching.
I would give you hope, but your hope is your own
unrealized dreams.
I would give you vision, but my vision can never be
your vision.
I would give you peace, but peace can only be found in
your own heart.

Then what gift could I give you at Christmas?
I would give you the gift of my mother, my father, my
sister and my brothers,
The gift that is the giver of all other gifts,
I would give you my love.

Some Men Once Thought

Some men once thought the stars were holes in their
bowl shaped haven.

Some men once thought they had to sacrifice to the
Gods when the sun moved toward the south in the
winter so evil spirits wouldn't take it away altogether.

Some men once thought the earth was flat and the end
of the world was a terrible edge.

Some men once thought the sun moved around the
earth and the earth stood still in the center of the
universe..

Some men once thought we could never soar through
the sky on silver wings.

Some men once thought our origin was different from
the other animals.

Some men once thought the species were immutable.

Some men once thought we could never understand the
chemistry of inheritance.

Some men once thought we were unique among the
life of earth.

Some men once thought we could never leave our

Reflections

home, the earth, and touch the stars.

But we have learned different!

I wonder how much we swear by every day is really different?

I wonder how much we swear by every day should be different?

I wonder how much we swear by every day could be different?

Who has made the difference? The ones who have been willing to challenge their tradition.

Let us all strive to make a good difference, for all Earth, and all life on earth.

Through the vision of the ancients we have begun. Let us continue!

Oh eyes! Oh hands! Oh minds! Oh hearts! Oh soul! Oh vision of a better world. Teach all men's children your ways. Give us the gift of your mother, your father, your sister and your brothers. For our mind set is formed by the first of our teachers, and our visions are born in the household of our childhood.

Our Moment

We have been with life from the beginning, for life
is an unfolding and we have ridden with it, passing
from soul to silent soul over the countless ages. We
all have a window of expression, a microsecond in the
unfolding of time. What we are we have borrowed, for
we are part of every life from which we have taken
substance for body or soul. We will give it back as our
window of expression closes: Our bodies to the Earth
to renew its life and the essence of our life and soul to
the spirits of life's children.

His Church Can Be Found in the School

The Preacher said:
The judges have ruled. Yes! They have proclaimed
it! For the benefit of all in their wisdom they rule!
The church cannot be in the school! What a sad and
deplorable rule, our church cannot be in the school!

And all the Preachers said:
Amen!

But the Teacher said:
The Master's church is well in the school. It lives and
breathes in the school!

And the Preacher cried:
But the judges have ruled! They have proclaimed it!
They have ordered it all! The church cannot be in the
school!

But the Teacher said:
What judge has jurisdiction over matters of the heart
and the soul? The church is all well in the school!

And the Preacher said:
What foolishness! What man are you to suggest such
a thing? A man of that heretic Darwin I'll bet! Our
doctrines are mute in the school!

And the Teacher said:

DUANE BROXSON. THE TEACHER

I know of your doctrines. I have seen them and felt them! Some have fashioned my soul, but many are truly mute as some were in the days of the Masterful Servant. Some speak no more for the spirit as they did in ancient time for they are lost from the reality of the ancient age that gave them birth. Their ancient image is lost to the clearer reality of our own age. Through their visions the ancients have seen and guided us. But through our clearer visions now, we must reflect upon the past and see into the future! First we saw with a blurred and dim image as if at a distance and even then we gained insight! What more as we see clearer now?

And the Preacher exclaimed:
I knew it! I knew it! You have said it yourself! Our doctrines are mute in the school. Our church cannot be in the school! Tell me! Tell me! I demand it! Where find I my church in your school?

And the Teacher said:

The Masterful Servant has spoken:
"A new commandment I give unto you, That ye love one another: as I have loved you, that ye also love one another. By this shall all men know that ye are my disciples, if ye have love one to another".

Sir: Where love is found in the school, there you will find your Master teaching as He has through the centuries. *His* church is well in the school, for many have loved in the school and you have never seen or known it. He has touched the hand of a handicapped child. He has wiped a tear from a heartbroken child's cheek. He has held them in his arms, grief stricken, over the deaths of their loved ones. He has jumped with joy with them for a concept grasped or a battle won. He has corrected them with loving rebuke when their hearts have failed them. They have cried with him in his own grief. He has loved them when all else, even you, have sometimes failed him. Go out and see our Master teaching! You will find Him in the classrooms, on the playgrounds and on the athletic courts of our schools. You will find Him there touching the hearts of our children! *His* church is alive in the school!

And all the Superintendents said:
Amen!

And all the Principals said:
Amen!

And an Old Fat Math Teacher from Texas said:
Amen!

Echo of the Bones

Oh dry and sun bleached bones!
I tramped the trails of life with these bones,
Teacher of the Lion, Hyena and Jackal,
I watered with you at the water hole of plenty,
I stamped with you the dry river beds of life.

I know these bones,
They were our rock, our helper and our guide,
For us you stood and cowered the threats of our blood drenched
land.
Where are you, oh flesh and Spirit of the sun dried bones?
Come, we must go, oh bones. Come! We must Go!
We must tramp the trails,
We must move, for moving is our life.

Arise! Arise, oh bones,
Come, come with us oh bones,
We must go! We must move!
Come, come with us, we must go!
We must tramp the trails,
We must move, for moving is our life.

We stand together on the graveyard of life's slain.
Teach us oh spirit of the lovéd dead,
Teach us in death a walk of righteousness.
Teach us with your visions, hopes and dreams,
Teach us with that ghost of immortal soul,
Oh speak within our hearts again,
And "tell the tale of where we come from and what we do."

Oh quantum spirit of the living dead!
The graveyard lives!
"Come from the four winds, oh breath,
And breath upon these slain that they may live."
Oh vision! Oh immortal hope!
Breath upon them that they may live,
Oh sacred bones,
Oh memory of the soul of life![3]

---

[3] This was written after viewing the strange behavior of Elephants over the bones of another Elephant on a National Geographic Video. I know the view is anthropomorphic. It was written that way purposefully to counter some of the criticism given to anthropomorphic views from a scientific viewpoint. This was the emotional interpretation of my own self as I viewed it. I know the Biblical quote was not for the actual bones of Jews to be raised but symbolic of the rebirth of the Jewish Nation. A view of the hope that decedents of Jews would arise again to form a nation and bless the people of the world. We see the Nation even now, let us hope for the blessing!

　　　　　　　　　　　　DUANE BROXSON. THE TEACHER

Our Prayers Can Be Heard in the School

The preacher exhorted in righteous indignation:
No wonder all hell stands to rule! Our prayers can't be
heard in the school.

And all the people said:
Amen!

But the Teacher confessed:
I lashed out at them! They were so purposefully
disruptive and inattentive, asking foolish questions
just to sidetrack my thoughts and desires for them.
One in particular, and with my years of experience
and knowledge, I isolated him, and scolded him, and
scolded them. So they questioned me, and cried out
in rebuke and contempt, all of them, as they made
their objections known. "What can I do?" I thought
to myself. So I stood before them and prayed in
silence to the God[4] of my spirit for their souls, and
for their impenitence of this rude and disruptive
behavior. As I prayed, I became closer and closer to
the will of my God as Its Spirit in dwelled me, and my
emotion and intellect moved me to the depths of its
possible understanding. Like a vapor, my animosity
and impatience and anger began to evaporate away
from deep inside me, and the pleasant peace of that

---

[4]All that I am capable of comprehending as "righteous" in this conscious world of will and
chance.

Holier Spirit began to indwell me, for my prayer was answered, only in the reassessment of myself. For I looked out among them and loved them, and in that instant, they saw me, and caught a glimpse of my deepest intent and the change that had in-dwelled me, and they stopped their objections, and in silence they listened, in spite of my words, to my heart.

And that Holier Spirit that can indwell us said:
Amen!

To The Senate[5]

Most honorable and distinctive men of the Upper House,
Noble men of dignity and power,
Keepers of the nation,
Holders of the pen of decision,
Wielders of the stamp of approval.

Have you not served our Nation?
Have you not consecrated her honored halls?
Have you not bowed with reverence in Her sanctuaries?
Do you not serve with dignity and respect?
Can you not stand with chance and will and call yourselves great?

Who are the poor and disgraced but despised wreckers of the
Nation?
With them go the worthless destructors of liberty.
They stand not among us as keepers of the peace.
Give them their due! Seal their fate! Cut them off from the body of
the elect!
Unclean! Unclean! Away from us, lest you corrupt us all!

Is it not the ranting cry of the self-fulfilled even in our midst?
Is it not the rhythmic beat of their war cry in the Nation?
Oh war cry of divisiveness and destruction!
Oh breaker of the heart, and spoiler of the brotherhood of
goodness!

---

[5]This was written during the time of the impeachment of President Clinton, and the debates over the direction of government and the Nation.

Can self righteousness be the rallying cry of the nation,
And judgment the healer of its wounds?

Come! Oh come, oh Spirit of that cross held Soul,
And teach us once again,
About prodigal sons,
And widows mites,
About rulers of darkness,
And Princes of Peace,
About blind guides,
And a publican's prayer,
About rich young rulers,
And becoming a servant.

Oh Grand Old Body!
Sustainer of the Nation!
Body of the most honorable and free,
Do more! Do more!
Restore to us the Brotherhood of the Nation,
Restore to us the oneness of American purpose.

Reach out! Reach out!
Sustain us with your compassion and understanding,
Sustain us with your benevolent heart and fairness of justice,
Sustain us with that bipartisan bond of American spirit,
Sustain us as restorers of the Brotherhood!

Then will your light shine out,
Like beacons to the people!
Then will your hand be raised,
Like the symbol of the Nation!
Then will your sanctuary ring,
With the joyous cry of hope!
Then will you also become,
"The healer of the breach".

To Janine Girl Baby

A tall sycamore stands
Like a towering giant
Beside a humble home,
Where grace and peace
And love abounded.

It stands like the arm
Of the Lady Liberty,
Proclaiming freedom and love
To all that have crossed
Its doorsteps.

You have crossed those doorsteps,
And all of the power of
That goodness goes with you
Now and forever.

Let that power lead you
So you never despair,
Never grow bitter,
Never lose that love and grace
And willingness to give.

For it is the willingness to give
That God sees,
And He empowers that soul
That possesses it,
That will not let the burdens

Reflections

And evil of the world
Destroy it.

It is in confessing,
That we are heard by God.
It is in forgiving,
That we are forgiven by God.
It is in giving,
That we receive from God.
And it is in loving,
That we fulfill the will of God.
May God bless you and keep you,

Dad

To Jerri and Chester Ladner

On viewing the thank you card, "Simple Back Yard Pleasures", by David E. Doss

I feel the summer sun shining on the paint peeling drop board siding and catch the fragrance of the potted flowers in the barrow. There's a window there, one to look in as well as out. I've raised it many times, and smelled the drying wood that sometimes binds the window in its jam. I've rolled the barrow, poured from the hand held sprinkler, and built the small bird box.

My heart is in this scene, scene of long ago but in the memory of the soul today. My dad affixed those flaking boards and plumbed that jam and casing. My mother scrubbed those rugged boards and washed that window sill. Is it the peeling paint, or rusting wheel barrow, or bent and greying can that revives the spirit and brings a tear? No. It was the pure and kind and loving hearts that, though in need, made us rich. Made the peeling paint, and sticking window and rusting barrow beautiful and longed for. For to me, Solomon in all his glory and riches, was not worth as much as this to me.

It is the love of God in the hearts of the loving kind
that fulfills the will of God, not a doctrine, not
a law, but a spirit of the mind and heart, A New
Commandment.

Love to you always,
Duane

It Troubles Me Not[6]

Sometimes knowing is a bitter blessing. Not in knowledge but in the changing of the colors and form of the foundations of the reality we have built from previous thoughts and dreams. From the act of a personage like man in our visions, to unexplainable acts foreign to our present models of our world and selves. Now, we just see what was always there more clearly, and catch our world in another light. But the essence of our struggle is not out there, just deep within, as it has always been. We are part of that unexplainable void of violence and energy. From it, the possibilities of ourselves was formed. We have been no more alienated by seeing it anew. We are both creation and consciousness and all of the unexplained nature of the heavens is what has "sent" us here. A part and partial of it all we are. God is a spirit that lives within us, coming from the essence of the stars we're made from, flowing through the eternity of the universe to be expressed here and there as you and me. And if the perfection of that spirit manifest itself in you and me, we would be in the Father and the Father in us, and we would know the Son and abide in His love.

---

[6]This was written in response to the line in President Carter's poem, "Considering the Void" because I thought I knew what was troubling him.

To America

I will lift up my soul and cry aloud unto the hills!
Where is my righteous father,
Where is my righteous mother,
Whose blessing flowed into my growing
Heart and made it sing?

Are you here and singing still, crushing as with a sword
The evil hands that would reach to do men harm?
Lift, as it were a cloud, the evil off my anguished brow,
And make the sunlight pure and clean,
The rain as fresh and clear as crystal glass,
And turn my eyes toward the purest blue,
And bathe my soul with Holy wind.

Where are you, oh my mothers?
Where are you, oh my fathers?
Oh come and wipe the darkened clouds off my sky,
And quench the raging fire within my heart,
And set my spirit right and make my passions pure!

Renew me oh my hearts of spirits pure,
Who walk amid the fire of tortured souls and vain desire.
Make your spirits known and cleanse me form the wrath
Of souls afire with selfish greed!
Reach deep within your faithful hearts,
And quench with Holy water the evil hell
That pours its searing fire upon the hapless children of our
land.

Shame! Shame! Shame!
Shame! Shame! Shame!
Corruptors of the vision of our children's hearts!
You whang and twang upon your instruments
A song that leads to hell the children
Of our righteous fathers our righteous mothers .

Shame! Shame! Shame!
Shame! Shame! Shame!
You rape the minds of their innocent hearts,
And plant the seeds of a devil's hell!
A devil's hell for fancy's knell,
A devil's hell for ding dong bell,
A devil's hell your wicked spell,
A devil's hell the sex you sell!

Shame! Shame! Shame!
Shame! Shame! Shame!
For love of money and a name
You play your selfish deadly game,
No thought of minds and hearts,
You lame and shame!

Where are you, oh my righteous fathers,
Where are you oh my righteous mothers,
Keepers of the purity of our innocent child deep within your
soul,
And teachers of the purest truth that sets our hearts aright
And makes our faces smile?

Shame! Shame! Shame!
Shame! Shame! Shame!
Sacrificing innocent children on the altar
Of selfish pleasure and blind greed!
Purge with hyssop as of old our hearts
From the tragedy of such insolence!
Return unto us, oh Father, the righteousness of our children's
mothers,
The righteousness of our children's fathers,
So their light will be not dimmed,
And their souls be not sacrificed,
On the altars of their father's insolence!

Oh, Beautiful! Oh, Beautiful!
Your beauty is in the spaciousness of your heart
As well as your land.
Where is that heart of yours, oh mighty America?
Where is that brotherhood of righteousness
And kindness and mercy?
Where is that hand reaching to lift the downtrodden?
Where is the purity of your passions and your heart?
Oh, for a moment with the memory of my righteous fathers,
My righteous mothers.

Oh, move our hearts to find again
The beauty of your hope,
The beauty of your caring,
The beauty of your kindness,
The beauty of your helpfulness,
The beauty of your fairness,
The beauty of your justice,
The beauty and majesty of the souls of your people!

DUANE BROXSON. THE TEACHER

Turn our hearts from the selfishness of a devil's hell
Reveling in money and pleasure,
And resurrect our righteous fathers,
Our righteous mothers,
In the consciousness of your masses,
And keep the fire of our hope alive!

Then will your light shine again as of old,
Like the beauty of your first morning,
Like the brilliance of your first day,
And meld all nations together with you in hope!

Then will your sunset be prolonged
Until the final setting of all suns,
And your joy will be full,
Your beauty pure,
And your spirit free.

To Israel

A faith without works is dead,
It is a sterile seed.
A faith without love is dead.
It profits us nothing.
A doctrine without His purpose is futile.
It tarnishes the soul.
A proclamation without His Spirit is irrelevant,
Like the image of an idol.

Nobler than the kings of many nations
art thou precepts oh Israel.
More precious than the gold of temple walls,
Holy art the visions of your Spirit,
Blessed art the promises of your fathers.

Oh Nations! Pay tribute to the author of
our righteousness
From their visions born of old have flowed
the Holiness of our God.
"Go forth! I will make of you a Nation." He
proclaimed.
"Go forth! From your precepts I will touch
the heart of man."

Blessed is the Name given by the spirit of
your calling.

DUANE BROXSON. THE TEACHER

With a contrite heart, they morn the house
of Him who has redeemed them.
From your sorrow and lamentations He
has touched their souls.
The redemption of your Nation shall be
their sign.

This was His promise from the ancient
times of old
This was His promise, oh dwelling place
of God.
Oh Israel! Oh Jonah! Oh sign of the Master
Servant
Why are you bitter? Is not salvation from
your God?

Yet still, your hope is in the Spirit of that
sign
Yes! In your deep despair, He has sent His
Servant!
His Beloved One, His blood will wash away
your sin!
His Soul has cleansed the hearts of nations and
with His Spirit he has humbled many lands.

I am the child of your rejection
Calling from the resurrection of your dead,
I am your offspring,
Lamenting with the Spirit of your Soul.
Oh bleed, oh bleed, oh beauty of my Servant!

Reflections

Crucify the wicked wretched evil of my soul!
Rebuild the broken walls within my heart,
And touch my spirit, even with the hand of
God!

Where, oh where can we find you now, oh
Jonah?
Sitting bitter under bough of withered vine?
Flesh of your flesh calls to you,
Spirit of your Spirit beckons you.

Read, oh read, my beloved people,
Read, oh read, in the doorway of your hearts!
His writers who captured with a stroke His
Pleading Spirit!
His writers who could not carve an image
Of our God.

Your promise through the ages still stands Waiting,
Your hope for future time is proclaimed sure,
It is written "You shall not always turn away"
For He has come to make your hearts His
Dwelling place.

Arise! Arise my beloved Israel!
Embrace! Embrace the Spirit of your Servant
Child!
Yes! Your proclaimed child of old!
Yes! Your Holy one!
Yes! Your redeemer of the heart!

Amen.

DUANE BROXSON. THE TEACHER

To Jerusalem

Stop! Stop now and harken unto the voice of righteousness,
The voice, cleansed with the fire of righteousness,
Calling from the mountains and hills
Embellished by Holy shrines,
Weeping in sackcloth and ashes,
And remembering in utter despair.
Hear His Holy word moving,
Speaking in profound regret,
"What a disgusting sight to all mankind!
I see the cold dead bodies of rebellion against only Him."

Oh slayer of the Jew,
Oh slayer of the Arab,
Oh slayer of the Christian,
Oh slayer of mankind!
When will you stop your slaying?
Oh Jerusalem, Jerusalem!
Jerusalem in tears by your hand!

For what does our Lord God call,
And for what does our Lord God demand,
That we should be called His people?
A spear through the heart of offenders?
A sword as the keeper of His will?
His disgust is the blade of the sword!
His rejection has called the marching armies!

Cry out the reverent praises!
Oh hear! Oh hear! The Lord our God is one God!
Make clear the profound proclamations!
God is only one! God is Great! God is Great! Long live God!
Speak forth the moving testimonies!
Jesus is Lord! Jesus is Lord! Jesus saves!
But what does the Spirit of God within us desire from the hand of his
people?
For what does It beg?

I hear the longing cry of our Servant, Prophet, Savior!
We see his pleading will for all mankind.
None are left without His promise!
He stands weeping at the sepulcher
Of His Holy Fathers!
Oh Jerusalem! Jerusalem!
House of Jehovah, of Ala and of God!
Stumbling still
At the truth of His righteous Will!
Oh let the light shine
And clear our clouded minds
For the praise of our Holy One!

It is Love not doctrine!
It is love more than martyrdom!
It is justice for the poor more than ceremony!
It is kindness rather than rebellion!
It is brotherhood rather than hatred!
It is to join hands not swords!
It is giving more than taking!
It is others more than self!
It is tolerance more than custom!
It is to relinquish and thus to save!

DUANE BROXSON. THE TEACHER

His hope is for your hearts!
This is His Jerusalem!
When will we ever learn?
Rebuild the broken walls
Within our hearts
For all mankind!

Hear! Hear all who long for justice!
Hear the word of Him who touches souls
With the majesty of His Spirit!
What would He have you teach
Your precious children,
The ones we cry for,
With deep and moving lamentation?
Hatred for all men,
In a false claim to glory?
Hatred for the children of our father Abraham?
Territoriality and selfish pride?

The child becomes the mirror of our own hatred.
We paint the pictures of his soul!
Look! Look deeply through that mirror, oh men!
Humble your hearts and turn to your God!
Worship Him in spirit and in truth!
And then you will find you cannot teach
Your child to hate,
Even a Jew,
Even an Arab,
Even a Christian,
For God is Love in us all.
Oh precious day!
Oh come with haste!
Oh precious day!

Reflections

Uncle Jim

I was just a child
When my Uncle Jim died.
We heard about his ship
That sank off Salerno
On the old radio.
We all sat around and cried.

Granny hoped that he was saved
But the Telegram finally came.
Only five were found alive,
One blown right over the side.
All the rest were doomed,
Especially those in the engine room.

Isn't it strange about names?
I've known many Jims.
Jim Booth, Jim Thorp,
Jim this, Jim that.
But Uncle Jim, this Jim,
Was like you had said
Another name.
The emotion and feeling
All deep down inside,
It just wasn't really the same,
To my granny, almost a holy name.

Granny never stopped hoping
She would see him step
Through her door.
What a man that Jim.
I feel the emotion now
As I sit and think about him.

I know that's why
They treated me such,
They said he loved me much,
And all of his love became mine.

And yes, there was Aunt Noreen,
His new bride we'd never seen,
Her grief was much,
And she came to visit us.

Much later on,
After she went home,
Back to Boston I think,
She wrote my granny
And wanted her graces
Over a man she was
About to marry.

What character,
Older times older people,
In my memories of home
And much more,
Oh I wish, how I wish
Like my granny before,
They would walk through my door.

Reflections

The Ballad of Whit and Duane
It Was More Than Fishing

*My father loved
to catch the trout,
But the trip was more
Than that, no doubt.*

*A lesson in
The strength of will,
Echos through
My memory still.*

*A home place where
They loved and lived,
By the creek,
Down under the hill.*

*It emptied soon,
Into another stream,
Where boys became men,
And my father dreamed.*

*A crystal creek through a basin swamp
Of cypress, juniper, and pine,
Over curving holes twenty feet deep,
We would cast our line.*

*My dad would skull the flat nosed boat,
Through runs and basins we would go,*

DUANE BROXSON. THE TEACHER

With powerful arms and rhythmic time,
Its bow would rock too and fro.

Skull he would, up the swift creek,
We'd go for miles and miles,
He'd never tire, or if he should,
He'd still skull for a while.

Moving close, next to the bank,
We'd see an otter slide,
And watch him slip down in the creek,
To catch a fish, his prize.

We'd watch real close for the gator's eyes,
We knew he'd be right there,
My dad would reckon up his size,
He'd give us both a stare.

He'd watch me fish and catch a bass,
Then we'd jump for joy,
I'd pull him through the swirling grass,
And he'd say "Hold him boy!"

That skulling job, he'd never quit,
And surely I knew why,
I'll keep it in my heart and soul,
Until the day I die.

Oh no, he'd never quit,
And all the men knew too,
Not one man on this river land,
Could match the things he'd do.

Down the creek he'd ride pine logs,
His peavy in his hand,
When they'd jam up on a curve,
He'd set them free again.

With a crosscut saw, he'd down a pine,
Then shave it with an adz,
The crossties cut were slick and smooth,
The best ones to be had.

With juniper trees he'd work with mama,
And split them with a fro,
Draw them down with the sharpest knife,
She'd stack them in a row.

To sweat and never whine,
To tire and no one know,
Up the creek we'd go.
His job, to get me there.
His will, I'll get you there.

My heart and soul confirm,
This lesson here I've learned,
I'll never quit on those I love,
My name is Little Whit.

My turn now, I'd watch him cast,
His every throw just right,
Right over the jutting stumps,
Right by the swirling grass.

Working the bait right off the bank,
I'd watch him get a strike,

A Jack fish lunge would take the bait,
A back jointed river Pike.

Right and left the fish would go,
Then up and jump, he'd shake the bait,
His red gill flashing,
Through the wake.

My dad would play him
On that line,
He'd show his green side,
Slick with slime.

Dad would catch him
Through the gill,
Oh my goodness
What a thrill!

There's in my mind
And soul today,
A memory proud
That won't go away,

A humble man,
Strong and brave,
That in his moments,
To his son gave,

A will to strive,
And not give in,
To things that crush you
From within.

Reflections

It was more than fishing and my daddy knew,
So here's a word from me to you,
I'll never quit on those I love,
My name is Little Whit.

In The Presence of God

Out across the yearning, hoping, crying, rejoicing
souls that are joining in the spirit with the resonance
of the holy songs and lifting up their hearts to reach
out and touch the hand of life, the mosaic cross brings
scenes of righteousness rushing through the air in the
memory of the mind. The varnished wooden beams
vault the ceiling toward the heavens, where the heart
unites with the spirits of the souls that silently sit below.
What emotion seems to flow from the dazzling colors
that surge through the mosaic window of the cross.
The golden yellow and orange warms the heart in
exaltation and in hope, while the red spills the symbol
of Christ's saving grace across the beams of the sacred
cross. I feel my longing spirit in the background of
the blue, a melancholy, a yearning for the compassion
of the Christ. And yet, as I look toward the cross, the
sunlight brightens with magnificent glory through the
glass, as though the spirit of Christ would bless us and
shine upon us. And as it dances across the singers in the
choir, the mystic colors touch each one upon the head
and baptizes them with the joy of Christ's saving grace.
Surely a blessing has come to my spirit, for it joins with
theirs in worship of the Christ, and songs flow forth as
a triumph for my soul. I know the Lord is there for I
see it in their eyes, and feel it in my soul, and the purest
compassion of my heart joins theirs in worship, in
worship of the Christ, Gods messenger of love.

Modeling for Nina Fritz

A Moment's Pose

She set my pose.

I sat upon a stool and gazed across the mall corridor at a beautiful lady in the window of a shop.

"Who is this man?", She must have thought, "What can I see of him in the expressions of his face?"

My mind was empty at first, months and years of emotional heartbreak had dimmed the light in my soul.

"This man is interested in my life, my work, my talent and my art." She may have thought. "I will let him see a little of my work. I will give him a little of myself.

I glanced for a moment into her eyes, perhaps to see a glimpse of her inner self.

"Look past me." She said, "or I will loose my concentration."

I knew my will was strong and my soul was filled with grand visions of hope, they had always been there. I reached down for her, to bring them out of the abyss into which they had fallen.

She measured with a squint of the eye and a mark of the rod and began to set my dimensions upon the canvas.

DUANE BROXSON. THE TEACHER

I anchored my pose with the trifocals of my glasses against the face of the lady across the way. What a pleasing young lady with a bright smile and the freshness and boldness of youth.

Surprisingly, she removed the canvas and turned it toward me. "This is not you yet."she said, "Just the shape upon which I will try to capture your features."

No I thought, It is not me yet, just the general form as she said, and I am not what I really am yet, but there is still time.

Back to work she went with a wide brush. I could see some of the stroke of the brush, but not its effect. It was hidden from my view. I was beginning to relax with the beauty and smile of the young lady. I contemplated the need of my life in her, and how I had missed so many times. I had so much to give, so much, and I wanted to so much.

She was more relaxed and not so intent as she built the foundation upon which the image would form. She removed the canvas and turned it to me. "This is still not you." she said, and explained how she had laid down the underlying base shades upon which she would catch my essence.

It was about then that music began playing in the background. . I began to find myself in the moving and wistful andante of the powerful base tempo. My visions moved out over the great expanse of the Gulf of Mexico as the basses moved powerful thunderstorms across the horizon. I watched the gulls sail along the melodies as they played in the foreground of the basses and storms.

Reflections

"Now, she said, I will use the small brush to capture your features and your feeling with the oil. I saw the concentration and intent to features and expression. I saw her squint to remove bothersome detail and unveil the essence below. She would find me with her oil.

From the expanse of the horizon, the music moved the ocean waves toward the shore where they crashed upon the beach sending up a misty spray. The cellos and bases drew up a darkened cloud and from the pounding waves I heard a beloved man cry out, "You will answer to God for this!" My soul shuddered as waves crashed over me. "Oh lift me Holy God!" I cried!

The lady's smiling countenance moved within the mist and crying birds, as earth's life force pounded out a will, a desire, a Holy hope within me. One that had always been there.

I saw her start to make a stroke, I thought, but stopped. "It is you", she said. I watched her scrape up the formless oil from which the visions of her soul had made my likeness. I saw a man outside the shop look at me and nod with a smile of approval. I moved down from the stool and turned to look. I knew for a moment in time I had found myself again. And lo--- she had baptized me with her oil.

A Prayer From the Heart
Sacred Heart Chapel
1/08/06 7:15 pm

Sustain me oh my Father,
Uphold Thy Spirit within me,
Stand by me, humble my silent accusers
And help me to love them.

They mock me for a weakness,
But my strength is in Thy righteousness,
It is Thy Spirit I have loved and none else.
Thy Holy Temple is my Joy.

It is not for evil I have wept,
But for Thy Spirit in Your dwelling place,
That Its' Truth in me might be known by thy people,
And the Joy of Thy Salvation be seen in us,
Even in me, thy servant, and the one who sings before me.

Amen.

I Am Poured Out

Oh Lord,

I am broken like the pot shards lying on the Holy Hill,
I am poured out, spilled like fine wine before the Bride of the Lamb
of God.
Yet in my despair, Your light still shines within me,
And the fire of Your righteousness makes me whole.
Restore my soul, Oh my Father, and let its light shine,
That I might find joy in Thy company,
And favor among the people of your tabernacle.

DUANE BROXSON. THE TEACHER

Honor Unto Death

"On the first day at Gettysburg, nine color bearers died carrying the regimental flag of the Twenty-fourth Michigan Regiment. During the same period, men of the Twenty-sixth North Carolina Regiment saw one comrade after another assume the crucial role; When darkness fell, their tally showed that fourteen color bearers had been shot." (Civil War Curiosities, pg 176)

Who were these men lying dead on the battlefield of Gettysburg? We know the Generals and the Presidents, but do we know them? Yes, we know them, for they are ourselves, the struggling masses of humanity. Their mothers and fathers wept and loved ones lamented, but male-kind forgot and turned its head, deaf to the fault within its soul! . A fault? But here on these pages of war is the honor and heart that makes men love to die— to commit the heart and soul to the point of death. "Oh flag of our countrymen! For your honor we would die!"

"Ye must be born again"---------- to redirect your honor, redirect your commitment, redirect your willingness to die. A sacrifice for a hope of love in the heart of man. Yes, a heart, a hope, a love, a vision— to quench the selfish fire that honors war. An honor unto death to end all war. O war, where is thy sting? O war, where is thy victory?

Reflections

A death to end the war within our collective selves. A death to purge our selfish selves and magnify our love. Can we rally around the cross as once our flag?

Hope For a Holy City[7]

I dreamed I was standing by the Holy Wall on the
Holy Hill in Jerusalem. Crowds of all kinds of
people were all around. I could see Jews with their
yarmulkes, Christians with their bibles, Moslems with
their kuffiyehs. There were others there, people from
countries all over the world who had come to view
this Holy killing place called Palestine. Yes, even
Jerusalem, the Holy Killing place of not only the body
but the soul in a Holy Land of war. Yes, Jerusalem, a
living oxymoron. My heart was poured out, my vision
broken like pot shards lying on the Holy Hill, my inner
being began to cry with a loud voice in the languages
of the peoples that had gathered there. It reverberated
off the wall of tears and hope, echoed through the
Dome of the Rock, and flowed out across the Holy
Hill of Calvary as if a Holy Wind had taken it there. I
began to preach with the deepest essence of my being.
I saw my Holy places flood through my mind, the
Belandville road, the woodlands, the farmlands, the
hamlets, towns and cities, where I had searched for the
Holy God in my soul, where I had become a man of
sorrow acquainted with grief. I cried out with a loud
voice:

Stop! Stop now and harken unto the voice of righteousness,
The voice, cleansed with the fire of righteousness,
Calling from the mountains and hills

---

[7]This writing, "Hope For a Holy City" is part of a larger writing, "The Flowers of Spring".

Embellished by Holy shrines,
Weeping in sackcloth and ashes,
And remembering in utter despair.
Hear His Holy word moving,
Speaking in profound regret,
"What a disgusting sight to all mankind!
I see the cold dead bodies of rebellion against only Him."

Oh slayer of the Jew,
Oh slayer of the Arab,
Oh slayer of the Christian,
Oh slayer of mankind!
When will you stop your slaying?
Oh Jerusalem, Jerusalem!
Jerusalem in tears by your hand!

For what does our Lord God call,
And for what does our Lord God demand,
That we should be called His people?
A spear through the heart of offenders?
A sword as the keeper of His will?
His disgust is the blade of the sword!
His rejection has called the marching armies!

Cry out the reverent praises!
Oh hear! Oh hear! The Lord our God is one God!
Make clear the profound proclamations!
God is only one! God is Great! God is Great! Long live God!
Speak forth the moving testimonies!
Jesus is Lord! Jesus is Lord! Jesus saves!
But what does the Spirit of God within us desire from the hand of his
people?
For what does It beg?

I hear the longing cry of our Servant, Prophet, Savior!
We see his pleading will for all mankind.
None are left without His promise!
He stands weeping at the sepulcher
Of His Holy Fathers!
Oh Jerusalem! Jerusalem!
House of Jehovah, of Ala and of God!
Stumbling still
At the truth of His righteous Will!
Oh let the light shine
And clear our clouded minds
For the praise of our Holy One!

It is Love not doctrine!
It is love more than martyrdom!
It is justice for the poor more than ceremony!
It is kindness rather than rebellion!
It is brotherhood rather than hatred!
It is to join hands not swords!
It is giving more than taking!
It is others more than self!
It is tolerance more than custom!
It is to relinquish and thus to save!
His hope is for your hearts!
This is His Jerusalem!
When will we ever learn?
Rebuild the broken walls
Within our hearts
For all mankind!

Hear! Hear all who long for justice!
Hear the word of Him who touches souls
With the majesty of His Spirit!
What would He have you teach
Your precious children,

The ones we cry for,
With deep and moving lamentation?
Hatred for all men,
In a false claim to glory?
Hatred for the children of our father Abraham?
Territoriality and selfish pride?

The child becomes the mirror of our own hatred.
We paint the pictures of his soul!
Look! Look deeply through that mirror, oh men!
Humble your hearts and turn to your God!
Worship Him in spirit and in truth!
And then you will find you cannot teach
Your child to hate.
Even a Jew,
Even an Arab,
Even a Christian,
For God is Love in us all.
Oh precious day!
Oh come with haste!
Oh precious day!

I heard the words "Blasphemer!", "Hypocrite!",
"Heretic!" "Infidel", as some in the crowd charged
toward me. I felt the stones beginning to pelt my body.
I cried out louder and louder, "It is love not doctrine!"
"It is love not doctrine!" "Love is real!" "God is Love!"
"*God is Love...*" as a large stone hit me squarely in
my temple. I stumbled forward bleeding and broken.
My mind faded into a glorious sunrise filled with mist
...... And I found myself, standing before the altar of
my church embracing the woman of my spiritual soul.

Oh Jesus Lord

Oh Jesus Lord, my feeble hands are reaching,
To touch your robe of the whitest snow,
And there be cleansed of all this earthly evil,
That meets us here as we journey through,
That meets us here along life's pathways,
And tries to take away the love you gave,
So till You come, oh Jesus help me carry,
The love of God, the love of God in my heart.

Oh Jesus Lord, my heart, my heart is yearning,
For you to walk with me on this earth,
And hold my hand amid the stormy trials,
That I will face on my journey here.
And be my guide through all the sky blue summers,
And be my guide through heartache and despair,
And lead me on toward that light in heaven,
That you have surely lighted for me there.

And now oh God, I place my faith in Jesus,
To cleans my soul of its' darkest stain,
To lift me up as even He was lifted,
From death's dark dungeon on that glorious day,
To be my crown of life and hope and mercy,
To lead me to the place where loved ones dwell,
And let me see amid the lights of glory,
The blessed Lamb of Calvary.

When The Black Man Sang Holy

I traveled forty miles one day to see my cousin,
To listen to the last rites of his death,
In a church he had help build with his brothers,
And where his family came to lay him rest.

I drove up to that church there that evening,
White columns stood like patriarchs of God,
I passed by to the doors of the chapel,
Through which many a seeking pilgrim had trod.

I walked inside the great chapel glorious,
I had come in honor of the dead,
Its ceiling rose up toward the heavens,
And pews could hold five hundred souls it's said.

The people were all standing around my cousin,
By flowers sent for loved ones in respect,
And on the raised platform there above them,
A magnificent burnished harp had been set.

As silence fell the harpist began playing,
The songs of God were soothing to the soul,
I could grasp a picture there of David,
Plucking its strings in a Holy Place of old.

On the platform sat two white men and a black man,
I wondered which would read and which would teach,

About the burden of death from great loss filled with grief,
In solemn honor of the family which would preach?

Then slowly to the pulpit walked the black man,
With emotion he looked inward for his God,
I knew he sought a blessing from his master,
In my heart I know I saw him give a nod.

From his voice then flowed a beautiful compassion,
A moving love song from lines penned of old,
In those moments I saw Christ in the garden,
Praying for the healing of my soul.

As he sang I climbed upward toward Mount Calvary,
And touched the blessed cross there of old,
And my master said, "Yes son, your wrongs are pardoned,
Just go on forward and be bold."

Aren't we all in this world just his children?
It matters not the station or the call,
Brothers, just kinsmen and brothers,
Oh why can't this be the message for us all?

I saw Christ in the face of that Black Man,
Through his voice, Christ was singing in my heart.
What more can any sinner live for,
But for God's work he should be a part?

And one day when I meet with God in Glory,
And the troubles of this world have passed and gone,
He'll say, "Yes, I was in the spirit of than Black Man,
And came and touched your selfish, suffering soul."

Reflections

I was there when the Black Man looked to heaven,
I was there when our Master gave the nod,
I was there when the Black Man sang Holy,
I was there, and I gave myself to God.

DUANE BROXSON. THE TEACHER

The Resurrection of the Soul

Once the light of Heaven that radiates from the soul,
reflected itself off the magnificent beauty of a Holy
Sanctuary. From the Cross to the lofted ceiling,
it resonated with the vision and hopes of spiritual
visionaries of old. In communion with the souls of
spiritual seekers all around, the Holy songs from the
yearning minds of old, lifted the heart to spiritual
highs not experienced in the realm of selfish desire
and selfish intent. But this longing of the heart was
not known by all. Some questioned and mistrusted
the intentions of its' presence there. "We know you
they cried." secretly in their hearts. "The sinful son
of the world and that is your home, perverting the
worship with sensual desires and selfish intentions."
"Oh no!", some cried openly. "We are all sinful sons
of the world. We must cast off our desires and become
one with the spirit of love and understanding. Yes, it
is sinful desire that corrupts the heart, but who can
know the desire of the heart without knowing the one
who possesses it? Who can know it without seeing
the outpouring of his soul? And yes, who has not
experienced it himself? And besides, he is not hers and
she is not his."

Worship dimmed to the flickering of a flame as the
suffering soul searched himself for evidence of their
claim. And yes, it was there and yet it wasn't. Out of

the purity of a searching heart and yearning spirit a forbidden desire was looming. But no, this was not the driving force of the soul. This was not the promise by the enlightening spirit that had visited him. What it promised was holy in every way. What it promised was a road to righteousness not vain hope in evil desire. Surely it was a purging of the soul by the act of an angel, and he knew this angel. What grief fell upon him for himself, for his Church, for his witness, for Christ, and for the angel sent from God.

"Oh my soul, I am dying with grief!" "No my son, you are not dying with grief. Grief is purging your soul as with hyssop and lifting you to a new spiritual enlightenment. You are dying to the selfish desires that force men's hearts to fail and I am dying with you or I have not died at all. "Then hold my hand." "Yes I will hold your hand, but not to death, to the resurrection of righteous desire and holy heart that you yearned for in the beginning. I am in you and you are in Me, and she is in Me, and I and the Father are One. Together we will go and meet Him on this Earth in the hearts of His children. They will know Me, and I will know them and they will see you with me and know you and will embrace us." "Take not only my hand but the essence of my being." "Oh my son, I Am the essence of your being, and we shall dwell together in My Father's House forever.

He Gave Me His Glove Today, Mama

Mother:
Where have you been son?

Son:
I've been over at Uncle Grady's house listening to the
ball games. We were listening to the Yankees and the
Cardinals.

Mother:
The Yankees and the Cardinals?

Son:
Yes mama, Uncle Grady had the Yankees on one radio
and the Cardinals on the other old radio that he has.

Mother:
Both games at once?

Son:
Yeah, he does that all the time. He says that this new
player Mickey Mantle might one day out shine Joe
DiMaggio.

Mother:
Don't count on that son. You know that DiMaggio was
one of the greatest players of all time.

Son:
He gave me his glove today mama.

Mother:
You mean that old first-base mitt of his?

Son:
Yes mama.

Mother:
You really love your Auntie and Uncle Grady don't you son?

Son:
Yes mama, but you know I love you all too, don't you?

Mother:
Sure we do. I sometimes wonder though if Uncle Grady loves us all as much as he loves those Yankees! Oh, you know I'm just talking now. Why, he loves us all as much as we love him. With your Auntie my sister, and your Uncle Grady your daddy's brother, it's like you have two mamas and daddies. They can't have children, you know. And your sister, why, they have helped us so much with her nurses' school. They love her so much. Yes, we are lucky, aren't we?

I'm proud he gave you his glove. It was special to him. Boy! Those Yankees, what great players! You know son, we have always been Yankee fans. I think it was because your Uncle Grady worshiped them so much. They have such great players.-. It won't be long now until your daddy comes home from work. We'll have supper when he gets here. You can tell him then how the Yankees did today.

Son:

Did you ever hear Uncle Grady tell the story about how daddy struck out all those players that time?

Mother:

Why yes son, I've heard that story a hundred times. Your dad was a good pitcher.

Son:

Do you think dad could have ever played in the Major Leagues?

Mother:

Who knows son? You know, after the eighth grade he had to start working. He has worked for his families ever since. He didn't have a chance to play any ball like that. Playing wasn't an option for him. But you know, he never minded because his family was the most important thing to him. Your dad is such a special person. He has such a love and respect for everyone, and yet he is so strong.

Son:

Why doesn't he go to church much mama?

Mother:

Well you know, growing up in the country like he did and working from day one just to have something to eat didn't give him much opportunity to come to town to church or anything like that. Church just wasn't part of his social life like it was in my family. Your dad possesses in his heart though, what some people strive all their life to find.

Son:

Reflections

Is that why everyone loves dad mom, even Mr. Gooden the colored carpenter that brings the saws by for dad to file?

Mother:
Yes, he is loved and respected by everyone. Your dad has a special heart. He is a special person.

Son:
Do you remember the day the Elders of the church came to visit dad?

Mother:
Yes son, I remember it well.

Son:
Gosh, I was thinking that day, boy, if they really knew my dad, he probably could have helped them understand what they were preaching better.

Mother:
I know son, but they meant well.

Son:
I'll bet Jesus would understand dad, don't you mama?

Mother:
Yes son, I know he would. His is the kind of love that binds us all together. This is the hope of the world son. That the love we have for our families and the respect and goodness that comes from it will someday be shared by all of the people of the world everywhere. You know, that they will be able to get along and have happy lives like we have. This was a hope of Jesus.

Son:

Mom, wasn't Jesus a Jew?

Mother:
Why yes son, you know that.

Son:
He was a great player too, wasn't he mom?

Mother:
Yes, the greatest, or else we wouldn't have people all over the world today changed by the memory of his teaching from so long ago.

Son:
How is that so mom?

Mother:
Because he tried to teach people to love one another by his vision and example, but not just their families, everyone.

Son:
Did he really rise again mother?

Mother:
They say he did son. But this I know for sure, God is a spirit that lives within us and every time that spirit of the love of Jesus finds its resting-place in the heart of a man to change his vision, Jesus lives again. It's like a nail from that Old Rugged Cross, driven right through our old selfish selves.

Son:
How can that be mama?

Mother:
From soul to struggling soul the flame of the hope of

Reflections

Jesus is passed and we purge our selfish soul with the vision of his love. His hope is for our hearts! This is His Jerusalem!

Son:
You mean the New Jerusalem, mother, that glorious view of heaven?

Mother:
Yes, the New Jerusalem. He said himself that the kingdom was within us.

Son:
Why mama, we've been there all the time haven't we?

Mother:
Yes. Yes son, we've been there all the time. God bless you son! I love you so much!

Son:
I love you too, mama.

Mother:
Enough of this for now, your daddy will be home soon. Why don't you go out and play a little baseball with the boys until he gets back?. And don't get those clothes too dirty out there in the field.

Mideast Challenge

The Great and All Knowing Spirit enquired of the
Masterful Servant about the nature of mankind and
asked: "By what name shall man be known among
the reaches of the universe that I might seek for him
all eternity of space and time?" And the Masterful
Servant replied: "I know of man. I have seen his
ways." And the Great Spirit said: "Tell me about the
ways of man" And in sorrow the Masterful Servant
bowed His Head and said:

"Men are:
Fearless fighting hating haters.
Wheeling dealing selfish seekers.
Laughing sassing lusting lusters.
Cheating concealing deceitful deceivers.
Lurking smirking lying liars.
Jeering smearing gossiping gossipers.
Plotting planning grudging grudgers.
Snatching stashing stealing stealers.
Whining writhing pitiful pittiers.
Harming hurting scornful scourgers.
Pious powerful exploiting exploiters.
Dastardly daring warring warriors.
Beating killing murdering murderers."

"But he has seen Me and I have loved him. And one
day I will be able to seek him for all eternity but My
time has not yet come." And the Great Spirit said: "So
be it my Masterful Servant."

Reflections

And the Spirit of Compassion said to me:
Speak a charge to everyone in the Middle East from
Ehud Olmert to Sarit Yashi, (not the writer), From
Mahmoud Ridha Abbas to the leaders of Hamas, from
the Imams of the Moslem world to the Palestinian and
Iraqi refugees, from the affluent and educated to the
poor and disenfranchised:

Purge this destructive essence of mankind that prevails
in guiding the people of the Middle East to their
ultimate doom!

I heard the voices of the people of the Holy land I love
saying, "Who are you?" And my soul said, "I am like
the voice of one crying in the wilderness, 'Prepare ye
the way'".

"Prepare ye the way", through mystical ruminations
to a supernatural spirit, apart from us, the view of a
Babylonian world of power and force, acting on its
own? Not for Him in this world!

Here the writer of old say, Get you out of the house.
I will give you a son in your old age. I will bless the
nations through the hearts and minds of your own
souls, through your children and your children's
children, by your own hand guided by the Devine
Force that lives within you. Yes! This was the call to
your Father Abraham, the call to the Jew, to the Arab
and through you to the world.

We will not be zapped by a supernatural "God"out
their somewhere. This God we seek is found within us,
as the Suffering Servant taught us. Out there is in here!

We are the heavens speaking! We are both creation and consciousness! From the throes of stars we were born! Would you have a "God?" Then God is "Love" for the salvation of mankind on planet Earth. Love does not look down from some lofty throne to play checkers with men here and there. Love is found and expressed in the hearts and souls of man himself! It is love that is Spirit and Truth!

Look! Look! Those Temple walls do not speak! They cannot hear the Muezzin cry! They cannot see the Oil on Aaron's Beard! Can these rocks reach out and breach the hell of man? They do not cry out an answer for your sorrow! Search the heart and make it sacred! It can speak! It can speak and lift the soul to touch the heart of God. Then will you feel His power in your will! Then will you see your Nations restored! Then will you see your borders relieved! Then will your love be known among the Nations! Then will their arms be stretched out! Then will your enemies be no more!

What kind of fool is this you say? What way can this be? Love them and die? Surely you cannot hate them and live, really live! Hate them for what? Walls that cannot cry out! Rocks that cannot speak! Lands that cannot know its possessor. Traditions that cannot hear your sorrow and your children's anguished cry!

From the grief and wailing of the Jew and the mourning crying rage of the Arab, the deep grief of my soul has cried out, has poured out its spirit to the essence that lives within. Speak it says! To which I moan, "Who am I?"

Reflections

*Binyamin Netanyahu is chosen by the Spirit of all
things righteous, he will lead his people. Not with the
sword only, will he lead, but with a compassionate
heart filled with vision. A sword will come and he
will wield it, but then, his mind will resonate with the
essence of the visions of old and compassion will fill it,
and all of the nations will be relieved. He will embrace
his enemy and they will embrace their friend.*

*Moqtada Al Sadar, the time of the terror is ended. The
voice of Death is no more. His disgust is the blade of
the sword! Yes! Even an American Sword! Make way
for the voice of the Heart and live! Lead your people
in the light of righteousness! Take up now the sword
of the heart for He has spoken of old! Behold! There
was a young ram in the bush and he did not thrust his
knife! It was not death He honored, but life! Life for
all! Your sons do not need to die! He has not called
them to die but to live!*

*What! Are you mad? How can you know? How can I
know, but that it came to me, in my grief and sorrow,
on the road to Sampson. Look! Hear! See now! The
Rocks do not speak! The walls do not cry out! Let
Him come and make your hearts his dwelling place!
Worship Him in Spirit and in Truth and your joy will
be full your Spirit free and terror will be no more.*

To Deborah

What does it mean to a man for a woman to be loyal
and faithful, to understand the big things and disregard
the little things? It is like the aircraft engine that you
bet your life on and the landing gear that takes your
slight drift on the runway. It is like the Sage that
knows the depths of your real heart, but understands
your human condition. Amid my consternation
over lost dreams and unattainable yearnings I have
always heard the quiet reassuring whisper, "I love
you Duane". No other woman has ever said that to
me so many times and meant it every time. I was
always the dreamer. The great adventure was just
over that next hill or beyond that sinking sunset. I
have been sometimes like the man who was looking
for a higher place to stand so as to gain a better and
grander view, and after looking all around, realizing
he is standing on the highest possible ground and has
the best possible view. No, not yearning to quit or
to break promises but just yearning, yearning for a
passed moment or an unrealized dream. Just yearning
like every man does, only with powerful feeling and
emotion. I have learned lately that the real dream is
already in my hand and the others are vapors that
evaporate with the burning rays of reality and the
constancy of daily devotion and commitment. We
have never sung a duet together but we have sung a
song of life together, a greater song, a profound and
powerful song, a song of family, of day by day caring

Reflections

and commitment, a day by day love song that is always there and is the real fulfillment of my most sought after dreams. Now I would like to draw you close and whisper in your ear, "I love you Deborah."

Your Imagination

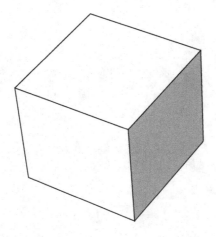

With your imagination, you can see into the flat surface of this page. With your imagination you can make the vanity of life beautiful.

From the bits and pieces of the ancient yearnings, mankind has, over the ages, with his imagination, built from them a beautiful vision, worthy to be upheld, for it is from the imagination and its visions that the "realities" of the future are built. These "visions" of holiness, stripped of their "territoriality of the mind set," mold and form for all mankind the inner workings of his societies in ways that make them beautiful for us and impart to them meaningful purpose for their future.

Reflections

Letters

May 3, 1992
Central High School
Route 6 Box 230

STEPHEN JAY GOULD, PH.D.
Harvard University
Cambridge, Mass.

Dear Dr. Gould:

I am a high school biology and physics teacher. I read many of your articles. I was moved by your article "The Most Unkindest Cut of All". I have written some of my own reflections. I hope you will not be offended or bored and read them all.

By what evolutionary mutative act does man's actions become unnatural? According to evolutionary theory, out of the primordial chemical soup, without conscience, came all of life's being to be called by part of itself, nature itself. Yet when nature consciously reflects on nature itself it excludes itself? Is not anything a man does natural? The concrete highways, the rising condominiums, the soaring spacecraft are unnatural acts of a natural man? What is this idea, "it's contrary to nature"? How can what it is be contrary to what it is? The extermination of eleven million Jews was an unnatural act because man's conscious will is unnatural? In its own horrible way it probably did affect the reproductive success of Jewish genes in some way. Our awareness allows us to select and choose behaviors both selfish and altruistic. Are behaviors objectionable to us, that is "evil", unnatural? Are altruistic behaviors unnatural? Is the will of man unnatural? Would Charles Darwin really classify that extermination as an unnatural act having nothing to do with his ideas of natural selection? Or would he have called it artificial selection because it was done by the hand and will of a man? Does madness, as you and I perceive it, act as an agent of natural selection? "What could be more unnatural more irrelevant to Darwin's process, than the intricately planned murder and starvation of several million people?" What do we do, exclude this horrible event from earth history as having no effect on the reproductive success of certain genes because man's will and man's moral behavior is excluded from the principles of natural selection and because man's will and its influence is unnatural? Is it Darwin's principle or nature's principle? I can see why the use of a scientific idea as the basis for justifying one's actions to do what mankind would call morally "evil" is repulsive. Mass murder, unfortunately, has been a "natural" behavior of man it seems for a long time. If by some power within the collective conscious man decided to eliminate all of the genes of a particular trait from the gene pool, that would be unnatural and have no effect on the reproductive success of the gene involved? If man succeeds in changing the flora and fauna of our world so that its outcome eventually excludes man, who will call it unnatural?

With selfishness afore thought man got a mind full of our ancestors law. We have always been alive as a life process since the "first life" and physically we are everything we have eaten. Every minute of every day the nonliving matter flows into the life process and becomes "living" and flows our of the life process and becomes "nonliving". The process is billions, if not billions and billions of years old and we were there. Not as an entity but a part of the process of the unfolding being passed on from generation to countless generation, from age to countless age. We must kill to live, whether it be a seemingly conscious less bean seed, a swift running deer or a filet mignon removed from the painful act of death by the "atmosphere" of the restaurant. All life possesses the same basic biochemistry. All of life's heart beats the same; the same carbon compounds of life, the same chemical processes, the same energy sources, the same Earth. I fail to see any guilt on the faces of the hungry hyenas as they consume the meal that sustains their life processes. Does the fish that eats its own offspring feel guilty? We have been programed by our past unfolding for self-sustaining survival. Out of the conscious less struggle for survival over the eons of time we have come to consciousness, bringing the triumphs of our past programmed with us. We are not new. We are a new dimension of the old to also be subjected to the rigors of survival.

When was it that man first realized the disparity that seems to exist in our situation? Was it when he ate the apple of his own self awareness and introspection and covered himself with the fig leaves of his own guilt? Was it when he ate the apple of his own conscious will to determine the outcome of future events? When did he begin to perceive this situation as salted with "good and evil"? A good man will love his mother and father. An even better man will love his enemies. But why feel guilty over certain behaviors? Does not guilt reflect our own realization of pain, suffering and sorrow in our own situation? Our own fear of pain and death and our own cries for caring and for mercy?

When I was a child, I killed wild birds with abandon, much to the chagrin of my parents. I can still visualize the terror and fear that some of these lessor animals suffered at my hand as I exercised the power of my own conscious will. And I have to admit, there were times when I felt guilty. Was part of it an innate hunting instinct? I see things differently now through the pain of my own consciousness, through the agony of my own heartache and despair, through the joy of happy smiles, happy hearts and loving souls. I would strive now to "harness the first and suppress the second". I really wonder sometimes if there is more than just a symbolic meaning to that passage in Isaiah: "The wolf and the lamb shall eat straw like the bullock: and dust shall be the serpent's meat. They shall not hurt or destroy in all my Holy Mountain, saith the Lord." Isaiah was aware of our plight on this earth. Isaiah used it as an exammple. Could there be more than just spiritual symbolism in the command; "Ye must be born again"? We must somehow obtain a new nature. We must "transcend the physical". Some how we must shed ourselves of some aspects of our old nature. But how? Will it be inevitable? What have we inherited? Is it a universal law, a unique flaw or just the "is" of our real world?

The selection of our physical genes finds its' realization at conception where it shades and colors the selection of our conscious collective selves, which extends from conception to death and overlapping, from generation to generation, transmitted by the interaction of all our learned experiences and emotional responses.

Why do we reflect with agony on some of the aspects of our conscious and unconscious struggle for survival? Are not lies the protective coloration of our own selfish selves and deception the tool of our selfish intent? Is it the pain of our ancient reflexes recoiling from the choices of our evolved freedom to choose, sustaining our ability to will as it has sustained our life force through the ages? And why do we view with swelling joy and gladness some of the aspects of our ancient heritage? Is it the pleasure of our ancient biological drives that sustain our life processes by their continued enactment? Is it the joy of fellowship, the gratification of insight and understanding, and the fulfillment of reciprocal caring and interaction that sustains the continuation of the conscious? Is it all of this unfolding in the tears of pain and sorrow, the laughter of pleasurable joy and happiness and the abstraction of the order of our inner working selves?

When I reflect on the success of "evil" in our own twentieth century, part of myself visualizes the watchman at the approach of the thundering chariots exclaiming: "And the riding is as the riding of Jehu", and I would by my own hand remove with power and force the "evil" in the world as I have viewed it. But my reflective self, my new testament within myself cries: "Behold the enemy 'evil' within yourself and overcome it by the power of the nature of your new self", suppressing the one and sustaining the other. Is it really a new self or just an evolving old self? Have I not acquired characteristics that I can pass on with the "genes" of learned experiences to other generations that can, in turn, acquire and pass on? Can I change by the power of my own will the nature of my inheritance that has sustained me over the ages on this earth? Can one refute with consciousness the very principles that brought one to consciousness? Is there a dynamic balance that favors the sustaining of the "good" and the suppression of the "evil"? Is joy and happiness and all that swells the heart more desirable than pain, sorrow and suffering at the hand of the selfish will of *a* man? Will the new orientation be sustained by the "nature" of things to come? Will it be realized by the conscious will of men? And what is *a* man but a moment in a grander unfolding of matter and energy in space and time?

The inspiration of science comes before the testing and as the result of it. It comes out of the curious, imagining mind of a man and is tested by attempting to refute it. Newton imagined a force and Einstein imagined a warped space field. By our own admission, ideas cannot be proven beyond some doubt however small under the circumstances of that day. I believe everything a man can imagine might be quite possible under certain conditions. All of our technological accomplishments seem to reflect to some degree our inner working selves. After all, isn't it our unconscious selves bringing us to consciousness as we attempt to explain? We are the up quarks, down quarks and truth quarks if what we imagine is really what we are. We are DNA to the "base" four and numbers to the base ten. But do we have the power to make some of our imaginings reality? Can we speak and make it so?

We can all imagine and hypothesize. I remember saying to a friend in nineteen hundred fifty seven, "One day we won't have to go through all of this. One day we will just turn on a gene and make us a new tooth right in the old socket. After all, we make two sets, why not three? Is there locked in the redundancy of our own DNA a videotape of our ancient past ready for us to play back on the video player of our genetic knowledge and computer technology? Was the ancient sun a binary that by some yet unexplained blow off and accretion produced the present sun and the debris that became the planets, asteroids and comets?

Hypotheses must stand the test of time. Some stand, some fall. The measurable, like the verse, melody and rhythm of a song, are part of the refutable hypothesis but the song in all its' fullness is the singers. Writers of songs give us something to test. If it is untestable now maybe it will be testable later. The singer of songs came before the tester of hypotheses.

Isaiah was a visionary. The vision of Isaiah touches the heart of many scientists. Isaiah affects science because it stimulates reflection and thought. It also influences how we use the knowledge gained through the refutable hypothesis. It helps power our visions and out of our visions arise the purpose for which we apply our science. Visions usually flow from what is to what can be. Some things that can be are fashioned from the power of an imagining mind in action. A Boeing 707 became part of the reality of the twentieth century from the yearnings and visions of the conscious mind of men. From the yearnings and visions of conscious man down through the ages were grown the realizations of the "better angles of our nature".

A few very keen observers and very profound thinkers have opened large windows of understanding regarding the nature of our universe and our place in it. Many have used this power for the "good" of mankind. Others have exploited the ideas of science to bring about selfish, destructive outcomes. I would like science for "good" to become part of the will of the masses of mankind everywhere, providing an unbreakable consensus that would counter the use of science for "evil" selfish intent. Selfish intent will surely manifest itself and seek to become the dominating force that fashions the destiny of the human race. The methods of "evil" selfish intent are clear and concise. They are part of our ancient evolutionary heritage both physical and "spiritual". The methods by which we can sustain the "better angles of our nature" are also part of our ancient heritage. Is not the "Law" the instrument where by we recognize and measure the degree of one's selfish intent? Did not the "Law" flow from the insight of the few, from individual to individual, into the collective conscious of the many, to be sustained by self reflective interaction with one another? And is not "science" part of the "Law"? What is the refutable hypothesis in the pursuit of a higher order wisdom and truth about the nature of the things around us, but the physical aspect of the same law that seeks to limit deception, falsehood and selfish intent in the pursuit of a higher order wisdom about the nature of our own interactions? Falsehood can be innocent but deception in the higher order of things arises from intent. Are our intents bound by the inheritance of our ancient past, programmed into our own physical nature? Or can they be reformed by the continued shifting of the dynamic balance toward the "better angles of our nature? Will the collective conscious ever realize the good man of "the good man and the evil", the essence of "The nine incapabilities", or the fulfillment of the "Law" by the enactment of the vision of Isaiah?

Men of science, can you allow yourselves to become separated from the visions that have established our spiritual "Law" and given grand purpose for the continued unfolding of science? Men of universal spiritual vision, can you reject with intent the insight of science and fail to be its' battle banner and fail to set its "proper" course and allow its' profound and powerful precepts to be used with evil selfish intent?

With our conscious mind we will will. And when we act on our will it will be so. Either for continuation of all our inheritance or termination of all our inheritance, it will be so. Either for what we call "good" or what someone else calls "good" it will be so. The outcomes will become "future history". Whatever we do, it will be natural, for nature is an unfolding and we are part of the grand unfolding in this small moment of a place in space and time. The "better angles of our nature " are slowly emerging from the conscious expression of our own will. How can we attain a love that passes all understanding? Will it be favored? Will it be sustained? Will all of the "evil" of our inner selfish selves be eliminated? They arrived at this moment in space and time together one sustaining the other. Is our consciousness just a flash of light in the darkness to be consumed by the darkness? The future is unfolding and we are fashioning a part of it by living in our own age and speaking in our own age. We must allow our "spirituality" to grow and evolve and become illuminated by our science and science to be illuminated and enriched by our "spirituality". After all, do not both visions proceed from the same imagination?

Good hypothesizing and may the better angles of your nature be with you.

Your friend in education,
Duane L. Broxson
cc James Wolfe PhD

Some Ideas Worth and Not Worth Reading

The process of energy transfer from one source to another flows profusely throughout the observable universe. The energy released as the result of nuclear reactions where the mass state is converted to the energy state and matter is transformed to radiant energy causes matter to be converted from lighter more abundant elements into the heavier elements of various kinds. Life seems to be entwined in all of the processes involving the flow of energy and the transformation of mater. The assimilation of the heavier elements and the carbon based chemical energy transformations are powered by the same process. One interaction leading to another interaction.

Under tremendously high temperatures, gravitation and magnetic fields, simpler structures are fused in stars into more complex structures. The star cycle that empowers the life process reaches a point where it can no longer sustain itself and the energy reactions diminish and eventually cease. Life proceeds as these processes proceed capturing the outflowing energy in the evolving complexity of the life process. Life results from a continuous flow of energy through the various processes that power the great stars of our universe.

Our life is the remains of the old powered by the fires of the more recent manifesting itself as an interaction of energy and matter. The great stars have a dynamic physical balance that defines their entity as their processes unfold. The star balance, however, is not maintained. It too is born, matures, grows old and dies. The universe seems to both form and consume itself wildly in the nature of its existence. As many as are "born" are the "deaths" as they throw off and condense the essence of themselves to be consumed in other processes. Many are the possibilities that arise. Many are the cyclic possibilities.

All life is an intricate balance empowered by another intricate balance. It arises, proceeds to its' level of efficient interaction, loses its balance and ceases to function. A life is a physical, and chemical cyclic balance that proceeds to the point of its most interactive efficiency declines and then dies. And if in the meantime a conscious will manifests itself as one outcome, dreaming, analyzing, determining, communicating creating, and interacting in a new order, is it not truly part of it all and not an intervention? And as this consciousness unfolds is it not part of the unfolding? What ever the result, will it not be natural? Our life is a natural unfolding of a moment in a place in space and time.

Do we not see the great unfolding of life on this earth? Proceeding from the throws of great stars and interacting with them to become perceived reality? Energy absorbing molecules transferring energy in chemical form were favored since the outpouring of the radiation of the sun was interacting with the various materials found on the earth. At the interface of earth and star radiation, enormous quantities of radiant energy bathed the materials there forming and degrading day by day for millions and millions of years. Eventually as the earth responded to these outpourings of energy, energy capturing mechanisms arose. But all earth was not continually bathed in radiation. Absence of radiation either by depth or cyclic night favored a different set of chemical mechanisms. Some processes were favored by absence of radiation and some processes were favored by radiation. Certain kinds of radiation favored certain kinds of reactions under varying conditions. The fires of the life process are powered by radiant energy capturing mechanisms which involve assimilation and degradation. Cyclic light favored cyclic life. Molecules frozen in the crystal state were not favored for the pulsating, responding processes of life. Neither were gaseous materials moving about more or less independently. Liquids were favored as molecule interaction suspended with these liquids were favored. Out of the flowing fluid of earth, oscillating and pulsating with the outpouring of radiant energy came life. Out of the essence of what is came what is.

Which came first the amino acid or the nucleotide sequence that interacts with it? Which came first single strand nucleotide or double stranded nucleotide? Amino acids and nucleotide were favored to be formed together under primitive earth conditions and hence their interactions were favored. Their interactions formed polypeptide sequences and nucleotide sequences which also interacted together, the one influencing the other. Out of these interactions came single strand nucleotide sequences which reflected amino acid sequences of polypeptide. By complexity, single strands precede double strands and naked strands precede coated strands. In any event many combinations and interactions of these forms occurred billions and billions of times in billions of places. Proteins interacted with nucleotide warping and forming one another under billions of different circumstances, responding to shapes in their larger structure and binding energies in their smaller structure.

The molecules of life assimilated by the energy from the sun became more varied and numerous. The chemical processes of the life molecules were sustained by the chemical memory of the processes that produced themselves. The assimilation of amino acids and the assimilation of the memory molecules occurred as the interaction of the one activated the interaction of the other. The memory molecules allowed the chemical processes to unfold countless millions of times proceeding in many directions and with more and more complexity, favoring those more consistently repeatable. Interactions with similar molecules became more numerous and complex. Processes of assimilation and processes of degradation occurred together in many possible ways and intervals. Interactions with dissimilar molecules proceeding along different courses and interactions with environmental conditions of a different kind were more probable at boundaries. Boundaries favored the sustaining of assimilating and degradation processes by interaction separation at interfaces. Boundaries formed interfaces favoring the formation of entities. Any mechanism which would make the exterior environment more interactively compatible with the interior environment would favor entities. Mechanisms providing molecules maintaining the preceding process would favor the entities. Assimilation and degradation of the same kinds of molecules whether structural, energy carrying or memory occurred. A boundary interface which allowed these processes to compliment each other favored the entities and sustained the entities. The compartmentalization and interaction at boundary interfaces favored the preservation of memory, integrity of structures, and continuation of opposite processes. Assimilation drew on structural, energy, and memory molecules. Since many of these materials were available only through the boundaries at interfaces, various mechanisms which favored the transfer of molecules favored the continuation of the entities. Obviously some involved the flexibility of the boundaries as a whole, out folding and in folding. Any mechanism which would offer some degree of "interactive control" over the external environment would be favored. Mechanisms which brought the outside inside and vice versa, by either passage, infolding or out folding favored the entities. Nucleotide availability from sources inside and outside favored nucleotide assembly. All single and double stranded molecules may not have become "degraded" to nucleotide either inside or outside. Some strands and pieces became incorporated into the entity memory. If favorable the entity would continue. If not, the entity would become itself part of the mix of pieces being interacted. These kinds of interactions could have occurred billions of times. If a piece was favored by an entity and incorporated into that entity, it would again be favored after degradation of that entity by similar forming entities. Pieces with expressive function at one period in the entity state could possibly progress, retained within the entity to a point of expressive non function by the nature of the unfolding sequences and the unfolding entity. Transfer of double stranded molecules that remained intact from one entity to another would mean that by sequence or existing chemical state that piece missed degradation. Molecules that close and bind strands were favored because binding favored retention and retention was either non expressive or favorably expressive, since unfavorable expressions would disrupt the entities. Incorporation into existing double strands was functionally favorable it became a piece with the "potential" to be similarly favored after degradation and cause the same changes. Mechanisms which rendered these "transfers" more reliable were favored. Elaborate systems for the transfer of double molecules arose.

Interactions within entities favoring entities preserved entities. Those that did not disrupted them. Boundaries internal and external that favored the integrity of entities and their processes allowed some processes to proceed and others not. Interactions at the boundaries that favored entities preserved entities. Boundaries themselves became a kind of programable process boundary memory. Boundaries became programed to accept or reject, that is to be discriminatory, by countless billions of trials and errors. Programable boundaries (that is boundaries that could be later modified) became constantly retained and constantly assimilated. External boundaries formed the space dimension that could contain and sustain the entity by balancing its interactions with the external environment. Life is sustained by interaction at an interface.

Double stranded molecules favored the repetition of synthesizing mechanisms. Since their double strand held in locked memory the form of the activating processes molecules up to that level. Single stranded memories in the naked expressive state had no specific over all process sequence control. To have a memory is one thing, but to have the right sequence access to that memory (that is cyclic memory) is another. The more or less random accumulative expressions of the process of single strands, were not as favorable for dynamic entities (less than dynamic entities exist) as the more ordered and sequence capable expressions of the lockable and unlockable double strand interacting with the single strand. Accessible memory from double strands to activating single strands to locked double strands was sustained by the process stabilizing nature of the cycle. Since the total process is an unfolding and cyclic one the procucts of the unfolding continues the unfolding within a time frame. Since a translated single strand molecule is not the activating agent an interval, occurs between its formation and its end result. This action reaction interval favors the formation of many and varied locking and unlocking interconnections both within the entity and between other entities as well as separation of memory molecules from the activating molecule production machinery.

Single strands could influence double strands. Single strand memory could become incorporated into the double strand system memory. It had no expressive impact, however, unless the placement was favorable or unfavorable to the cyclic process in progress. Internal interfaces and boundaries were also sites of interaction and they formed boundaries. As the events within the entities unfold the chemical nature of the entity itself unfolds enhancing some processes and inhibiting other processes. The chemical unfolding occurs as a result of the expression of unlocked memory but after that event by a time interval. Surely degradation of processed single strands became part of the process and degradation products in part or in whole were either expressively favorable, expressively unfavorable or null. As the processes locked in the double strand memory unfold in entities it reaches unsustainable proportions as materials needed for assimilation diminish, as demand increases and concentration of favorable and unfavorable products increase, reducing the probability of surface contact by reactants and changing the chemical nature of the entity itself. The mechanisms established at the boundaries produced by the process itself become no longer able to sustain the internal processes due to the increased mass volume within and the decreased surface contact without. The most efficient interactive mass volume ratio would be favored. Boundary mechanisms through continuous interaction become less efficient and interaction memory loss occurs as transport molecules within the boundaries become inactivated. Entities cease to function and the process ends. These imagined sequences of events could have occurred billions and billions of times. The huge number of sequences leading to the eventual end of these entities, however, favored the chance happening of any mechanism which would cause the sequence to recycle. One that would restart the process and allow it to unfold once again. This process, though unlikely, out of the billions of "trials" and "errors" that might occur through chance, would only need to proceed by increments, each one bringing the entity closer and closer to a higher order cycle. It would sustain itself if it in fact reached that point since it is controlled by molecule memory. Herein lies some insight into the inter-working of

DUANE BROXSON. THE TEACHER

the life process and chance occurrences. Even though an event might have a very large chance of not happening all at once in the first place, the huge number of repeatable events due to the interaction of natural memory molecules, gradually over time, brought about the event. Subsequent events after the initial event might even be favored because of the nature of its unfolding in an energy powered cyclic process ordered by naturally occurring memory. Nature "herself" biases the randomness in the great outpouring of energy. Cyclic interactions are internally sustainable and objectively predictable. Underlying the predictable events are cyclic interactions.

The process that culminates in a single strand also by similar process produces double stranded copy of the memory molecule. Double stranded copy is sustained and retained since it increases reliability in the cyclic process possessing accessible process memory. How does it become accessible? By the physical products and cyclic nature of the chemical state of the fluids of the entity itself being directed along interfaces within time intervals as it unfolds and as it has unfolded by countless billions of "trials and errors". Many copies of the double stranded memory molecules would be less favored than fewer copies of the memory molecule since mass volume ratios would affect surface contacts and interrupted cycles would be favored. As the process proceeds with favorable additions to the cyclic process the underlying activating memory is retained in the double strand. The replication of double strands is completed when the chemical state of the entity has reached its historically old "end point" or potential restart point of the internal cycle. Continuation of the process by the renewed activation of several copies within the same entity would not be favored and would result in the same end point. As interactions with old boundary materials caused changes that became fixed in the boundaries the nature of "old" boundary material and "new" boundary material became different. Interactions at new and old boundary material were different as a matter of sequence in process and interaction. Mechanisms which produce infolding of boundary material were favored. Any such mechanism which also, by the nature of boundary production, associated itself with the attachment and separation of double stranded memory molecules from the rest of the entity would favor a renewed recycling of the entity's internal processes. This loss of mass recycling process would favor the formation of mechanisms which would effectively separate double stranded molecules. The physical size and configuration of these double stranded molecules. as well as their opposite orientation and variable chemical nature, distinguishes them within the matrix of the entity material and favors mechanisms of separation. Any mechanism which favored the separation of these double stranded memory molecules would favor restarting and any mechanism which would also cause division of the mass would favor restarting, allowing the process to proceed not to an end point but toward a division and recycling point. Preservation of the entity state by division of the entities favored variations in the results at the onset. Movements and out folding and infolding of the boundaries provided mechanisms whereby larger materials even other entities themselves could become part of entities. Entities within entities which were mutually favored by the cyclic processes, preserved both entities and added new dimensions to the activities and interactions. Variations in the products of entity division produced anomalous entities of various outcomes. These conditions favored the rejoining of entities and cyclic mechanisms of these kinds of interaction were favored. As the environmental conditions of the earth unfolded all of these cyclic phenomenon unfolded into more ordered and complex over all interactions. The randomness of the origin of the cyclic processes began to take on more order due to the interconnectedness of the selected cyclic mechanisms and the simultaneous programming of memory molecules all being driven by the outpouring of solar energy. Entities which existed under various conditions might rejoin other similar entities which existed under different conditions.

As entities began to reproduce themselves some necessarily became closely associated with themselves forming larger groups. Others did not. Those that did not were either dispersed or dispersed themselves by their unique ability to move about, however crude the mechanism. Since for entities protein production was a mater of programmed process, proteins with the ability to physically respond (that is to physically contract under certain chemical and electro-chemical interactions) to changes (stimuli) in the environment were produced over and over by various mechanisms. When one of these mechanisms gave an entity an advantage the mechanism was retained since the entity was favored. Memory molecules in the case of mechanisms of motion or motility were the initial instigators of the physical and chemical processes that began the cyclic process, however the cyclic motion mechanisms sustained themselves once begun (time intervals are very short) and were subject to changes in the surrounding environment and any feed back modulation mechanism involving memory molecules. Since motion involves energy expense, various cyclic energy producing mechanisms had sustained the motion cycles. Fluctuations in the process producing motion instigated fluctuations in energy producing mechanisms since the cyclic processes had become integrated. Various internal energy pathways along boundary interfaces developed. Highly specific interactions from the external environment could now instigate a change in the cyclic nature of the processes inside the entities. The extenal environment could in some cases, without disruption, modulate the cyclic energy processes within the entity. This led, by one route, to what later became "Sensation". Repetition of cyclic energy transfers along bounday interfaces literally billions and billions of times favored molecular imprinting of these various energy flow pathways. That is to say, that the nature of the repetitiveness occurring over and over produced physical and chemical changes in the entities that favored the sustaining of those pathways and those repetitions by their cyclic nature. Energy depletion might temporarily shut down the cyclic motion process only to be restarted through pathways already imprinted. Division of entities does not necessarily indicate the complete disruption of pre-established cyclic mechanisms. On the contrary, this sustains the process. These mechanisms might be passed somewhat intact from generation to generations favoring the development of feed back and modulation mechanisms within the entity itself. Energy availability could become an effective on or off switch starting and stopping cyclic processes.

Favorable responses favored the entities. Various mechanisms of response and movement unfolded that were imprinted into sort of functioning physiological memory pathways apart from the modulating memory of the double stranded molecules. Physiological memory pathways sustain the stimulus response mechanism. Energy transfers occur along physiological memory pathways, and may be modulated by external and internal stimuli. Continuous cycles involving the release of energy favored the development of many additional energy releasing mechanisms along physiological memory pathways. The development of these memory pathways unfolded with all of the unfolding through billions of internal cyclic repeats coupled in turn with billions of cyclic entity repeats. Since interface boundary material and internal entity material is conserved in each sustaining cyclic division of entities basic physiological memory pathways and programmed interface memory are also retained.

Homogeneous groups of entities developed and the interaction of the similar entities within the group being dimensional favored different sustaining mechanisms. Conditions were especially different for those of the group that were on the edges, on the boundary interfaces. Some mechanisms became expressionless under different conditions but remained locked within the memory molecules. Some mechanisms became null though expressed and degradation products became part of other cycles. As multiple entities increased in size and number the same conditions limited the continuation of purely homogeneous groups of greater and greater size. Out folding and infolding of groups of homogeneous entities were favored. Interac-

DUANE BROXSON. THE TEACHER

tion of entities at fold boundaries occurred under different chemical conditions and intervals affecting continuous physiological memory pathways and programmable boundary interfaces. Various responses to these different conditions separated by both physical space and time interval from initiating entities caused changes in the programable boundary interfaces both internal and encoding that affected the internal chemistry of the entity and effectively locked and unlocked aspects of the memory molecule. Specialized entities within groups of similar entities were favored. Specialization did not favor group selection by over-all division of the group. Mechanisms which caused the repeated division of the entire complex were muted by specialization. Within homogeneous groups memory molecules produced molecular structures which by nature of the interval of production and internal entity chemistry remained expressionless within that entity. Mechanisms already in place favored the movement of materials through the interface boundaries. Reaching entities of different chemical states where the nature of the interface boundary allowed interaction they found expression and the outcome was subject to fitness producing specialization. Billions of these kinds of occurrences developed chemical memory pathways involving entity memory availability, physiological memory pathways, and entity phase cycles and produced additional interface memory programs. Homogeneous groups folded and became "Specialized" along various pathways to also become subjected to the same tests of fitness. Homogeneous groups of entities specialized in various ways also favored the formation of specialized group boundaries.

As homogeneous groups of the simplest order were disrupted under the same conditions they proceeded to the same stabilizing point altered only by additions, deletions or changes in the interacting entities memory systems. However only those changes in the entities which could recycle the group were lasting for the group. As greater specialization occurred among the various groups of entities, specialization became so far removed in form and function that many

Letters

specialize entities when separated could not restart the group development process. However, entities which followed different more subdued courses might retain enough of their initial status to restart the group cycle. Remembering that many copies of the memory molecule within the same entity would not be favored and remembering that memory exchange mechanisms and fusion mechanisms were already in place for initiating entities, any mechanism which produced a specialization route that led to the reduction of memory molecules in large numbers of entities within the group, would favor recombination upon dispersal with other similar entities of similar groups and would also favor the development of a restart cycle. These interactions would favor groups as a whole, since they would produce diversity. As specialization became more complex these special entities removed from other entities of the group by location and the sequence of unfolding events became the only entities of the group that maintained enough of the initial state chemistry to reform a group either by itself or in combination with other similar entities of a similar group. Some of these entities of some groups could conceivably restart without recombination taking a different but similar developmental pathway only to recombine later with others of itself to produce variations of the original developmental pathway. Others might prove unable to restart the group, restarting only in combination. Changes in the memory molecules of these entities and their subsequent recombination with other entities to restart the groups provided variation in similar groups and favored the sustaining of those groups. More complex groups of entities do not recycle at the group level. They reach an end point. (death) Since the very specialized cells originated from the parent cells through a process cycled not by the specialized cells but by other parent cells the nature of their existence is a historical function of the imprinting of cyclic events and the repetition of these cyclic events in the actual unfolding of the group toward these specialized cells. The nature of some of the events which determined some of the changes in the cyclic processes of parent entities may be far removed in historical time

DUANE BROXSON. THE TEACHER

from the events as they occur in development, for the event which precipitated the development of a cyclic process may not be necessary to sustain the process after its start.

Before a zygote divides it interacts with itself and its external environment. However after its first division it interacts with itself, the environment (which has been more or less predetermined by the larger order of its kind) and the products of itself. After an interval cell structures can influence other cells in ways that were impossible while their own development was occurring and also more recent cellular elements can cause expression in parent cells that were impossible at the time of their development. What seems to unfold is a grand interaction of influence which proceeds from uniformity to great diversity as it interacts and unfolds throughout intervals which are determined by the very activity of the dividing cells themselves. Embryonic development is not only an expression of genes, but an unfolding of sequential events, events occurring under the influence of previous events, events modified by historical occurrences which instigated changes in retained cyclic processes apart from memory molecules. In other words, the genetic code in a zygote does not seem to code specifically the sequence of development as a property or order of itself, nor does it seem to control all of the activities of the cell The sequence of development is coded by "events" which have sequenced themselves by occurring in billions of repeats over billions of years of time establishing the intervals of cyclic events. This time interval sequence seems not directed specifically by the memory molecules other than being an accessible memory bank in the enactment of a "nature tested and tried" historical imprinting of cyclic phenomenon activated by the unfolding. The memory of the developmental process seems to be in the process itself.

Your friend in education,
Duane L. Broxson
May, 3 1992

January 20, 1993
Central High School
Milton, Florida 32570

SCIENTIFIC AMERICAN, INC.,
415 Madison Avenue
New York, NY 10017

Dear Editors:

Re: "How Should Chemists Think?"

I respectfully understand professor Hoffman when he says, "Chemists can create natural molecules by unnatural means", as he defines unnatural, but can it really be a matter of definition? When did man and the power of his conscious mind and will become unnatural? When did we become unnatural Promethean participants? Nature herself biased chance in the life process long before we became a conscious entity. The conscious mind is but a bolder expression of that same bias. Hands are natural and the conscious minds and wills that guide and direct the work of hands are also natural. Conscious thought and will have been brought into being by the same processes we call natural, yet when we reflect on the outcomes of our own interaction, we should look upon them as unnatural? We can neither return to it or surpass it because we have always been and are it. Whether we emulate or create, our activity is natural. The results of our activity is natural and will have its own natural consequences. In other words, it will be subject to fitness. The intent and will of conscious thought as an expression of the collective conscious is a powerful and dynamic participator in evolution. Consider only the endangered species. If man succeeds in changing the great cycles of this planet so that its outcome should eventually exclude man, who will call it unnatural?

DUANE BROXSON. THE TEACHER

We are not new. We are a new dimension of the old flowing out of our ancient ancestry as naturally as any other process. We have seen through the eyes of both Aristotle and Plato and we will continue to do so. We are the substance of the old calling into being the interactions of the new. We are nature itself forming and shaping itself in its continued unfolding. We have not removed our self from it by our own cognizance or by the recognition of our creative impact on it.

Out of our natural struggle for survival over the eons of time have flowed much of our destructive behavior and selfish intent. Out of our own self introspection and cognizant interaction with the world around us are flowing the insights that are quelling the unnecessary expressions of some of our destructive selfish intents. Ideas and knowledge find power for expression within the collective conscious. The essence of our creative ability exalts us and fills our souls with vision and hope. The magnitude of the exploitation of our creative ability for selfish reasons by forces within the collective conscious condemns us, blurs our vision and destroys our hope. We must gather to our hearts the ideals that have created our grandest visions and we must emulate and create with all of the power of our will to make our visions reality and the unfolding of the human species a grand and noble one. We should focus the power and influence of our scientific intellect toward the forces that shape and control the expressions of the collective conscious. The forces within the collective conscious that formulate its intent will speak and it will be so. Whatever the outcome, it will be natural, for nature is an unfolding and we are a part of it in this small moment of a place in space and time. Let us hope that the future the natural activity of man will cause to unfold will be found favorable within the great cycles of this planet and that the creative vision and hope of an unselfish human spirit will prevail.

Respectfully yours,
Duane Broxson
Teacher of Science

July 8, 1993
5882 Cedar Tree Dr.
Milton, Fl. 32570

AMERICAN MUSEUM OF NATURAL HISTORY
Central Park West at 79th Street,
New York, N.Y. 10024
Attention office of the Editors.

Dear Editors·

Re: This View of Life: "Poe's Greatest Hit"

Raw nature it seems has always been a taking, a giving (whether willingly or otherwise), and a sharing. Human culture brought about by
the interaction of man's conscious will is a taking, a giving and a
sharing. Raw nature? Why the adjective? Nature is not all black and
man's culture, as a part of it, is not all white. Why do we view man's
conscious will in contradiction to "raw nature"? Isn't it all a part of
the same unfolding? Has not science and literature flowed from the
same selfish and altruistic imagination? Isn't each day's science our
unrealized hopes imposed from within by our own natural selves?
Isn't our culture also a natural agent in our world having its influence
whether we include it in our rationalizations or not? Should we not
cherish the position?

Respectfully yours,
Duane Broxson

DUANE BROXSON. THE TEACHER

July 8, 1993
5882 Cedar Tree Dr.
Milton, Fl. 32570

DR. STEPHEN J. GOULD,
Museum of Comparative Zoology
Harvard University
Cambridge Mass. 02138

Dear Dr. Gould:

Here in Florida we have crows not ravens. I hope you won't view my lines in the same regard, as a crow and not a raven. I have included some of my reflections. I hope you won't be bored or offended and read them all. By the way, I am doing my homework.

Your friend in education,
Duane Broxson

Man the Sower of Seeds[8]

The love of the Masterful Servant, regardless of perspective, is a universal part of nature herself, unfolding as all nature unfolds, favored to be sustained in some form by the great unfolding of life within us. It cannot be denied for it has flowed with us unknown and unseen in our ancient past to be called to consciousness and amplified by the interaction of great visionaries. It will overcome the "evil" within us by changing the very nature of nature herself. Nature of yesterday has

---

[8] "Tis the Raven Nothing More" was included with these writings. It may be found in Reflections.

brought nature of today into existence. However, nature of today is not nature of yesterday. Nature of today will bring into being nature of tomorrow. However, nature of tomorrow will not be nature of today. Linked by the grand unfolding? Yes. But an unfolding in which each unfolding event thrusts forward the "nature" of nature. There is no predetermined future. That does not eliminate the prediction of future events however. Nature observes the tendencies within herself by the power of the conscious mind which unfolded with all of the unfolding. The power of the conscious mind, which is natural by the way, can change here and there the future unfolding of nature, because it is nature, and will do so. Future is now later. The chances that are possible now are not the chances that are possible tomorrow when that day comes. Attest to the past though for insight into the tendencies of nature. If altruistic behavior was not favored in some way or process it would not have become part of the "nature" of nature. Do we not see an increased disdain among men of all walks and religions for selfish behavior? Do we not see altruistic behavior being worshiped as a "true gnosis" by many? Do we not see the unfolding of nature? Sure it could be changed. But will it? Will we begin to teach hate and selfishness as a way for all men? I think not. It is too painful. After all has this not helped call into existence altruistic behavior in the first place? Every man for himself is really not favored in this chance interaction of nature. It ebbs and flows, but the dynamic balance seems to be shifted toward the altruistic. We murder a few in Bosnia Herzegovina as we did in Germany. But oh the heartache and pain that even the onlookers suffer as they empathetically relate their pain to their own, their heartache to their own despair. We starve a few in Somalia, but oh the heartache that the collective conscious has as it witnesses part of itself inflict such suffering for selfish reasons. And even now a few of us have even begun to love our enemies, that is, those other species with which we share this grand unfolding. Even now some seem willing to admit our oneness. Will we ever be able to share the insights we have gained in advance and to the detriment of our fellow species? Oh nature! Is your message really our

Good News?

The human mind is the great acquirer. When it comes into existence, it is not programed to a large extent. It acquires characteristics. It is plastic. Its power can influence others of its kind to acquire the same kinds of characteristics. The great acquirer has thrust itself forward. Nature itself has lifted up a decision maker, a purpose maker (even if just for self). Man and nature white and black? Nature is a continuum. It cannot separate itself from itself. With humility of hindsight (I hope) man will give all nature a mind full of his own acquired law. Can we not "tame" the animal (much to my disgust in terms of the circus)?

We have taken the world by the power of our own selfish force. Can we sustain our influence in it with our own acquired compassion and understanding? Yes, out of the great Lion of Judah has flowed insight of the great contrast, the great juxtaposition, selfish force to sustain our own selfish desires and great humiliating compassion fueled by insight and understanding for all of nature around us. In the great King (David) we see a balance of both, though one was directed more upward (to the Devine Spirit) than outward. In the Masterful Servant (the Jewish Jesus) we see a sowing of seeds of the shift of the dynamic balance. Can we doubt its influence? Out of the great Lion of Judah has flowed the compassion and will to sustain the interaction of the conscious (with our power and technology could not the wrong people at the right time end it all?) . We should cherish the continued suppression of the one and the sustaining of the other. Man has recognized his uniqueness in nature. Can he also recognize his oneness and by his action allow his "better angles" to be sustained? Can he integrate his acquired knowledge and power asserted by his will with the grand balances of his own birth? Will we continue to view man in contradiction to "raw nature" and not as an integral part of it , culture and all? When will we be fully able to accept the great insight of our twentieth century science and act upon it to sustain the better angles of our conscious nature which has been lifted up unheard and unseen through the bowels of our bare earth?

Duane Broxson

July 8, 1993
5882 Cedar Tree Dr.
Milton, Fl. 32570

DR. JAMES WOLFE,
928 Rural Street
Emploria, Kansas 66801

Dear Jimmy:

I have completed a few more ideas about various things that I thought you might like to read. I know to knowledgeable scientists these ideas are probably quite superfluous. I am interested in expressing my opinion about the direction science and philosophy take in the ensuing years. I have been doubly blessed in my life and I have tried hard to give back some of the gifts that were given to me. As I interact with students every day, it saddens my heart to think of the difficulty some of these children will have in the coming years if we fail to make the right decisions (if there are any real decisions that can make a difference) regarding the future of our society. I also realize in the next few years science will advance its knowledge and ability far beyond anything we might imagine. Many challenges will face the citizens of the next generations. Most of them will center around the exploitation of the environment, overpopulation, global economics, and energy. Many of them will involve biotechnology, genetic engineering and other controversial issues. Many will center around regrouping our religious philosophy and morality in such a way that a the people will be able to embrace the profound principles of science and also have a spiritual hope for a spiritual future. We must attempt to unite our collective conscious in such a way as to establish a feeling of oneness in purpose. It will require uniting our leadership, political, scientific, and religious. To put it in a way that can be understood, the men of science will have to sing the hymns of our spiritual visions along with the politicians, business men, laymen and children. What's more, they will have to sing in the same choir. Certainly I don't mean everyone, but a consensus. The spiritual aspect of man cannot be left out. Man will leave the science out quicker than he will leave out the spiritual. In a democracy we should know that the masses have clout. With a powerful and united leadership embracing both morality, ethics and science there is not a challenge we cannot meet, there is not a group that could not be eventually led. This is as frightening a thought as it is comforting for they must be led for the good of all people in a spirit of honesty and integrity. A corrupt and selfish consensus will be utterly destructive to the principles of the free will of men and the pursuit of happiness. I see that direction more and more each day. Science is going to place in the hands of men dynamic and powerful tools more frightening than nuclear arms. We will be able to fashion man in the image of our own preconceived notions. We must teach our society to fly before we give it the airplane or a mighty crash will ensue.

It is hard to replace a walk in a quiet wood with the spirit of all nature around you and the souls of your beloved ancestors calling to your heart pure and honorable visions that give you courage and strength and the will to make a difference, with a computer, many gadgets and a testable hypothesis. A society without a soul is dead. Science is a part of society. We need them both. I know the love, guidance and concern that your parents gave to you was a gift that motivated you to the high level of success that you now enjoy. I see children every day and I see young and eager hearts with much potential guided by love and concern. But I also see an unloved, troubled, emotionally starved, spiritually depraved, pleasure oriented, and goal-less mass, moving as if it were a stampede of Wilder Beasts towards who knows where and for who knows why consuming the products of our science as if it were the grasses of an unlimited prairie.

I sense the profound and deep knowledge and understanding of Dr.

Gould both in science and in literature. He has probably written more than I have ever read. I recognize his position and status in the scientific field as well as your own. What good are ideas though if they are never expressed?

Where am I left after all of these discussions? Probably untrained and foolish in the eyes of the real men of science and apostate in the eyes of the people of my heart. I will not reject the insight of science, and I still dearly love the people of my heart.

I have four children. Two from my first marriage that have their own families now. I have six grandchildren. My last two boys from my last marriage are Joshua and Daniel. Joshua is ten years old and Daniel is five years old. You can see, I stay busy.

Good luck to you and best wishes. I understand that you are moving to Mobile in the near future. Maybe I will see you again one day.

Your friend always,
Duane Broxson

August 24, 1993
5882 Cedar Tree Dr.
Milton, Fl. 32570

DR. STEPHEN J. GOULD,
Museum of Comparative Zoology
Harvard University
Cambridge Mass. 02138

Dear Dr. Gould:

I thought I would send you these few ideas in reference to the work I sent on "Ti's The Raven Nothing More". I know you are a busy person with many responsibilities and that you probably get many letters from unknown persons like myself. I hope you will find time to read them.

On The Evolution of Choice

Statistical analysis refutes desert coloration as due to chance. Statistical analysis refutes chance in the selection of peppered moths. From a different perspective, the bird biases chance with its selection pressure as it biases chance in its selection of food. What makes the bird seek moths for food? What motivates the bird to make choices, conscious or otherwise?

When the sun first began pouring out its radiation onto the newly manifested earth, the processes that produced energy sustained earth life began. The first molecules of life began interacting as an energy driven repeated-ness and was a bias of chance or randomness. The

DUANE BROXSON. THE TEACHER

beginning was a response of materials present to the availability of energy. This beginning interaction between life molecules and energy and between life molecules and other life molecules was the underlying characteristic of the processes that followed. As life forms became more complex, interactions of molecules and systems both within the life forms and between other life forms were selected as favorable or unfavorable. Favorable interactions were sustained and unfavorable ones were not sustained. The nature of the molecules themselves was the discriminator that mediated the "response" making. Even the simplest response or "affinity" could be viewed as a choice based on "experiences" encountered by the choice maker. A response in this case would be subject to fitness and would become an evolved choice. Surviving responses manifested in the molecular structures led to more complex interactions which were also selected as to fitness. As life forms became more morphologically complex, experiences initiating responses or "choices" became what we might call inputs into a system. The choice might have been to react or not to react, to react "positively" or to react "negatively". Membranes became selective receptors of input as a result of evolved choice. In this case, the membrane would have become the choice maker. Membrane memory in terms of selective choice was eluded to in a previous paper. In interaction between living things and with the nonliving world, both random and non-random inputs were received. Cyclic physical phenomenon also biased chance from some perspectives. To living things on earth the cyclic rising and setting of the sun biased chance along with the constant outpouring of energy. Based on input the organism responded but its response was peculiar to its own physiologically and morphologically selected history through organism memory like DNA, membrane memory, physiological memory pathways and etc. In responding , it literally made a "Choice" based on its own evolved existence since it had been selected by its experiences. Its response or "choice" also had its affect on future interactions of itself and the world around it. Over billions of years, in retrospect, feed back mechanisms (feed back mechanisms probably derived from energy pathways needed to power the response as eluded to in an earlier paper) developed ordered responsiveness, ordered choice making..

From this one can see that living things, whether plant or animal, conscious or unconscious, literally pick for their "craving" . They pick with their morphologically and physiologically evolved response history and continue to do so only if they are successful. They make favorable responses, "choices", based on their selected response history and programmed memory. Their systems develop elaborate programs whereby in response to the living and nonliving world they pick for their "craving". This act of "picking" is a result of and at the same time a driving force of natural selection as mentioned by Darwin. (When the picking poem was written, I did not know Darwin had ever used this word) This choice making, beginning very weakly and progressively becoming more intense and specific as living things evolved is the underlying characteristic that produced amplified competition between all living things at every level. Driving much of natural selection is choice making whether unconscious or conscious. It makes no difference. Like the birds it causes (allowed by Mayer) selection pressure in many ways.

At the earliest stages of multicellularity the selection pressures produced by entities were more similar than different due to the low level of specialization. This, in effect, produced a more homogeneous over all structure and function as an underlying stepping stone for all multicellularities, the cohesion of basic gnomes if you will. The gradual increase in specialization (an internal choice making interaction) at this point in time also gradually increased the tempo and specificity of competition due to the evolution of more specific choices and eventually led to an increased specieation as it produced the differences in selection pressure that helped to separate and fashion the further diverging gnomes. The physical environment sets the stage in the earliest life for the basic underlying structure of the life form. First life was more alike in all respects than different. Since interactions between life forms were also selective as to the course all life would take, these interactions proceeded from similarity in interaction to more increasing diversity in interaction as life's forms passed from similar cohesions of molecules diverging to species as it went through the hierarchies of structure and function of developing organisms. The evolutionary "choices" of organisms also became more complex and divergent and was functioning at all levels increasing the intensity and specificity of competition and giving an unpremeditated direction to the course all life would take. An acceleration of divergent interaction after a lag, if you will, as more specialization and speciation produced more diversity which produced more specialization and speciation.

Multicellular organisms increased in size, locomotion and responsiveness, propelling themselves through their environments. This ability to migrate, (multicellularity also allows for conservation of its basic internal environment as it migrates), allowed them to easily move into different environmental niches. These migrations however were not entirely random for the unfolding of evolutionary choice in their responsiveness had already biased their mobility to "pick for their craving", that is to say, to respond positively to favorable conditions or to respond negatively to unfavorable conditions and to "seek" out resources pressured by their heterotrophy. These migrations with their "directional" attributes favored the speciation of large numbers of multicellular organisms as they moved into the large scope of available environments and potential niches. The Precambrian-Cambrian boundary, (probably not as narrow as is now conceptualized), could be viewed as that time frame in the evolution of organisms where some multicellular diversity already established, macro mobility, aerobic energy mechanisms, and the expression of a higher level evolutionary "choice" resulted in more intense and specific competition and propelled an accelerated speciation period. Since photo synthesizers manufactured in citu much of their resources for life and development, mobility and mobility related responsiveness were not as potent a selection attribute in terms of fitness. This may help to explain the more diverse and novel forms of "animal" life in the great oceans, considering plant life as the photo synthesizers. This is not to say that the photosynthesizers did not develop a kind of responsive choice making system. We know plants respond. Their responsiveness was evolved differently and did not develop along the same mobile evolutionary pathway due to the decreased "demand" factors in their selection. Photosynthesizers were not as diversely interactive. They competed between organisms less for "food" than their more demand driven, mobile, heterotrophic counterparts. Indeed, in the beginning the presence of photosynthesizers may have somewhat reduced the selection pressure for mobility and mobility related responsiveness, augmenting the long time interval that occurred between simpler forms of life and more diversity. It was not until photosynthesizers colonized land that mobility mechanisms became strongly favored in plants, that migration became strongly favored, and great plant diversity developed. In the oceans necessary minerals were obtained through a mobile substrate. On land, the mobile substrate was absent. Competition and selection pressures produced more diversity as methods of dispersal developed for photosynthesizers. In fact the plants "cashed in" on mobility already established in the heterotrophs. Mobility and its related responsiveness certainly parallels the development of nervous systems. The development of mobility and responsiveness and the heterotrophy that favored it was the beginning of the long unpremeditated unfolding of consciousness. Something that plants, the photosynthesizers, seem to lack.

Survival of a species is only manifest in retrospect. It was not competition for survival but competition for their "craving" that led or did not lead to their survival. Life is a process that has occurred continually at an instantaneous moment. Perceived time only manifests itself as an interaction manifests itself in consciousness anyway. Life occurs continually but only now. It is brought to the moment by the past but the future is just a now, later. Only an organism looking back

DUANE BROXSON. THE TEACHER

into history or forward into prospective future can give meaning to survival. Living things do not compete for the survival of their genes any more than the first molecules had affinities for survival of the molecules. Survival of the molecules was the result of selection acting on the affinities, but survival can only be realized as a conscious mind contemplates it. Their evolved picking for their craving has brought them from the affinities of primitive interaction to the competition of the higher level now. They pick for their evolved "craving" which may or may not lead to the survival of their genes based on the outcome of their interactions as it has always been. Life did not occur with intent within itself, of course, but higher order intent has been manifested by the fundamental processes of life. Intent is in your words, "natures grand experiment". Will it be favored? Choice making is an essence of the interaction of life and competition. Will intent take us beyond totally destructive competition in the picking for our own selfish craving?

Perceived time became a reality only when conscious interaction became a reality. All events are simultaneous. Our observation of events cannot be simultaneous with the events being observed. Only an organism looking back into history or forward into prospective future can give consciousness to a process that only occurs in the now. Higher level choice requires anticipation. Our anticipation is established through remembered experiences. Our experiences and memory are ancient. They have journeyed through the ages from the uncertainty of contingency to ordered necessity within the life process on earth. As we view events with consciousness, in retrospect, projecting our experiences into the future, we conceptualize most of our craving as a "need". We may conceptualize some specific craving as an "endless aching need"! Consciously we need but the essence of life does not need. Consciousness is an interaction that stores, recalls and projects inputs from other interactions. An interaction becoming its own interpretation of other interactions from which it has received information. Essence though is instantaneous. No wonder we so complexly discern in the uncertainty principle what the ancients saw in their hearts. For essence that is instantaneous to be called to consciousness requires interaction storage and recall of past events in the now. To conceptualize it we must observe it first, but to observe it we must interact with it. "How should he know him by whom he knows all this?" Cognizance can only come from recall of the past unfolding in each now of instantainety.. Activities are so quickly executed that macroscopically we view the present when in effect we are reviewing the past. Measuring, being an observation, is an activity that requires an interaction and therefore an interval, making the measure of the essence unobservable. We live in the now but we record the past to bring ourselves to consciousness, for as we play our interpretations of external events we become in consciousness those events and based on them, we project ourselves beyond the now into the nonexistent but sure to unfold future. Since the nature of things is instantaneous, nature in the form of man looks back and looks forward and perceives itself. Since it is an interpretation that can also fashion from it an intent, nature has enabled itself to alter its own higher level interactions with its on evolved choice.

Go ye therefore, oh man! You are nature of all things itself, catching a glimpse of itself, but knowing self only through reflection of external interactions played back on the recorder of all life's soul, of which you know and can know nothing. There is no past. There is no future. Only now exists in reality. I am has sent us and it is the beginning and the end in the same instantaneous moment. Past and future are an activity of the conscious. The conscious mind, however, can project itself into the future and with its intent make choices in the now that lead to a predetermined outcome. Here in lies the power of a grand vision. Its power of suggestion can motivate an intent far beyond itself and, depending upon the strength of the intent, promote the realization of the vision.

I come to this moment with the spirit of all my experiences and reflections calling to my inner soul this day, as it has every day since I can remember: "Choose this day whom you will serve". And each day I have chosen, for myself and for the honor of my mother and father whose presence forever lives within me. Yes. We are culture bound, but there is an innate beauty in all cultures. Those who have experienced it also like to share it. Not a dogmatic religion, but a beautiful, good, and wholesome gateway to the "future".

Physicists produce more and more high energy interactions but get no closer to the essence of reality than the Indian, realizing his oneness with nature, calling to the great spirits of his own birth for the spirit of the deer he has just slain. Consciousness is always an imperfect second hand interaction. Yes. We see through a glass dimly. We chase essence into a collapsing black hole only to see it resurrected by evaporation back into the realm of the conscious. Life is mortal, but its essence is immortal, instantaneous and has no beginning and no end. "Twinkle, twinkle awesome star, I am a part of what you are".

Yes, there is it seems, indeed, an internal driving "force" of natural selection. It has unfolded through the life system and has become extremely elaborate. Through association and feed back mechanisms, it has produced consciousness, that is, an integration in an organism of inputs of the senses and internal body mechanisms, both immediate and historical, and the ability to choose its response in expectation of the future and in memory of its experienced history. This is why the assimilation of input data into human consciousness is so complex. Integration of the inputs developed as these systems came gradually on line in somewhat different time frames and then became more specific. The sense of body part presence and touch, I would say first. Its gradual integration into higher pathways had already begun when other systems started coming "on line". When we turn the conscious on, we engage the senses into the integration. We perceive with our senses for the most part our external selves through interaction feedback, but with their shape and form we grasp for expression of the unfelt, untouched and unseen inner being that has called us from our ancient sleep, and awakens us each day for the realization of our moment of a place in space and time.

Oh the pleasure of ice cream and loving friends! Oh the pain of a foot in an ant hill and the heartache and despair over a ruthless Washington! Picking for its craving also includes removing or isolating detrimental or injurious interactions. Responding negatively to input. The pain of an interaction. Pain is an associated detrimental interactive input that calls up a defensive response and has an evolutionary selected history. Pleasure is an associated favorable interactive input that calls up a positive response and also has an evolutionary selected history. Eventually higher organisms actively pursue their "craving". For example, they pursue the food that they like. They reject the food that they don't like. They avoid experiences that produce pain and they seek experiences that bring pleasure. I see my dog smile when I fulfill his requested expectation. I see my dog frowning, emotionally dejected, at my refusal and at my scolding. Anthropomorphic? Yes. But my dog and I have more common an ancient history than anyone in my neighborhood will consider or even let me talk about.

I think attention should be given to why organisms in specific ways pick for their "craving". How does this picking move them into different environments where interactions of chance and otherwise are different? Does a constant interaction between living organisms and the materials or situations they "seek" allow for the assimilation and incorporation of nucleic acid pieces and segments between different organisms? Could an intermediate chemical exchanged in the process alter the genome of the interacting organisms? Could there possibly be a transfer of a bit or piece of nucleic acid (not sexual in that sense) that might influence one or both, say, toward similarity? I wonder if investigators consider that the evolution of the mimicked and the mimicker could sometimes occur simultaneously. Tobacco plants can glow like a firefly now and *E. Coli* can produce insulin. An "intervention" some would view. A new strain produced by the "picking" of mankind. It is a new strain nevertheless. How does genetic transfer of DNA occur under circumstances other than sexual where the "craving", "seeking" activity brings specific, repeated interactions into reality? I think I know that *spirogyra* does not know it is exchanging DNA or that this produces another *spirogyra*. What makes the spirogyra respond to the other cell in this way? Did the "seeking" mechanism come before the exchange, and the interaction being so favored, was retained? Wouldn't sexual activity in humans take place simply as a pleasure seeking activity even if it didn't result in pregnancy? As a matter of fact, many today think of pregnancy negatively. Has sexual activity in higher forms of life predominantly evolved from a pleasure seeking activity that has a very good and favorable outcome? Was it a good and favorable outcome of responsiveness that also evolved into a pleasurable one, sustaining itself with positive feedback?

There is an aspect of choice making in some form at every level of earth life, for life is in essence an energy fueled bias of randomness. The human form and the human consciousness expresses to the highest level at this time on earth, that bias of natural randomness, not only within ourselves but also in all of our creations which are in reality extensions of our conscious and unconscious selves. It has manifested itself as a purpose maker, an organism with intent and will calling on the memory of its historical experiences both conscious and otherwise to see visions and dream dreams and to determine to some extent the course, as all life does, that nature will take. If we should try to exclude man from "raw nature" we should then exclude all life, for all life plays with dice and uses the same deck of cards.

Oh the joy of victory or the pleasure of a perfect steak! Oh the sorrow of the death of a child or father! Yes, from a similar event can flow both joy and sorrow. We are all of life's joy and sorrow, pain and pleasure, hope and despair in the realm of the conscious, but not by our own choosing. Yet we have become the purpose makers. We walk with intent. In the words of a man with stirring insight: "Verily you are suspended like scales between your sorrow and your joy. Only when you are empty are you at standstill and balanced." Could we say, "I have met the soul walking upon my path."?

Was Charles Darwin's hypothesis just an intuitive one? He had in his hand experimental evidence supporting phenotypic selection. He chose not to call that bit of evidence natural selection. He called it artificial selection because it was done by the hand and the will of a man, which he perceived as unnatural. I guess a Buffed Polish would never have become another kind of chicken if unnatural man hadn't intervened and changed the predetermined course of all nature and made it unnatural?

I really think it is an important difference. Yes. I understand the implications in regard to genetic engineering and the like. The fear of another Hitler is a real one. But the memory of heartache and pain like that sustains us and strengthens our better visions and dampens the chance that we would allow that to happen again. The agony of those experiences must never be forgotten. We must teach our children those lessons. We must write it on the doorposts of our hearts. I hear the expressions "tampering with nature". But when we really see that we are instruments of nature itself, maybe we can realize the importance of the natural actions we take insofar as morality and ethics are concerned. They have been caught up in visions and dreams but those too are natural. Maybe then we can really see that we are the purpose maker for "good" or "bad" and either one has a damn good chance of becoming reality, and science is not the only activity that determines the course of events. Consider politics. As a matter of fact, science has become a powerful tool of the collective politic used and controlled to a great extent by the politicians and entrepreneurs for their selfish purpose. Maybe we should put a lot of our scientific energy and intellect into understanding the origins and function of morality and ethics and the stabilizing effect they seem to have on societies. Maybe we should compete with the politicians and entre-preneurs in their own arena in order to influence them. I really think that the work of the men of science of all nations as a communicating body has had profound positive influence on the future of our societ-ies. We should recognize the importance of our great moral leaders and help them understand the powerful precepts of modern science. They should embrace new enlightenments. We should not reject them with arrogance.

A scientist must specialize to be successful for the most part. Their participation in the interaction of science with the great institutions of our society is limited by the demanding nature of their work. Out of necessity they isolate themselves in a work so specialized that only they or their kind can understand, and into which few of the lay pub-lic can hope to enter. Science must point to decisions that need to be made and take an active part in making those decisions. I really feel that the men of science, for the most part, and the men and women of the teaching profession are some of the most upright, moral and ethi-cal people in our society due to the nature of the calling they choose. One to discover knowledge and "truth" if possible, and one to create a desire for knowledge and "truth".

Man's science is a servant of his collective purpose. Let us unite our fragmented collective purpose with the power of our science and the vision of our hearts and propel the good of mankind from the uncer-tainty of contingency to the threshold of necessity and beyond. This we must attempt for it is becoming more and more obvious every mo-ment that the visions of "Weeping and wailing and gnashing of teeth" are well within the realm of possibility.

We look in retrospect at the unfolding of our old testaments and we see the joys and sorrows of the walks of all men unfold before our eyes. In a glimpse though, we see more. We see the activities of our own selfish selves bringing into reality much of the heart ache, sorrow and despair. But we also catch a glimpse of those struggling souls in the lives of their now, whose minds and hearts have poured out a vision in a grander nobler testament to be further realized in the far reaches of another now, that, being mortal, we too can help to unfold. Their heart beat can be felt in a paraphrase of the words of one of those immortal souls: "Behold, life is not dear that you may love life; but that you may love all life's self through life, therefore life is dear."

I stop and listen, and again I here the spirit of the Indian offering up his blessing for the gift that is his sustenance, knowing that one day he too will freely and willingly give back the gift that life had given to him.

Your friend in education,
Duane Broxson

December 5, 1993
5882 Cedar Tree Dr.
Milton, Fl. 32570

OFFICE OF THE EDITORS,
Natural History Magazine
Central Park West at 79th Street,
New your, N.Y. 10024

Dear Editors:

Re: This View of Life, "Four Metaphors in Three Generations"

I recognized an uncredited reference as a saying of Jesus concerning the recognition of good and evil deeds. I was a bit puzzled as to why it was used, considering its extended implications.

Many Christians cannot fit the principles of Darwin into the hopes of their faith. Some would even view Darwin's works as evil deeds. I feel sure this is one reason Darwin, in his time, postponed the publication of his work. In view of this, I offer these reflections:

How Reckoned are Deeds?

How reckoned are deeds,
In this land we do trod?
What some see as blasphemous,
Others as God.

We form what we think,
By how it is viewed,
Both in offering it up,
And as it's construed.

Some swear by Sir Darwin,
A truth there achieved,
But some that love Jesus,
Refuse to believe.

Some see in loved Jesus,
A beautiful seed,
While also in Darwin,
A masterful deed.

In search of sweet truth,
Take your hats off please,
For those that would reckon,
The fruits of both deeds.

And what could I offer,
For lives so sublime?
Only one looked forward,
One backward in time.

Duane Broxson
Teacher of Science

December 5, 1993
5882 Cedar Tree Dr.
Milton, Fl. 32570

DR. STEPHEN JAY GOULD,
Museum of comparative Zoology,
Harvard University
Cambridge Mass. 02138

Dear Dr. Gould:

We have learned through science in this century that creation, (that is, what we perceive to exist), is the creator of the processes that have brought into being the consciousness we know. Our understanding of the life processes has shown us this. Therefore, in this respect, I am has sent us, for I am both creation and consciousness. How this relates to the great I Am, as each views each speculates.

Science and literature cast serious doubt as to the ability of consciousness to perceive the essence of itself, since it is and is within the system it is trying to perceive. Einstein's quote has intrigued me from my youth and I have given it much thought. Mind (consciousness) is not matter, its embodied essence that we recognize in other non-living physical things, aware of itself, but an interaction of matter and energy becoming an interpretation of other observed interactions. We are aware of certain interactions of itself but not of the essence of those unconscious interactions within us that are common to all creation. All causality is brought to conscious view by past experiences. Mathematical equations are symbolic representations based on past observations and experiences and the logic that has been deduced from those experiences. The parabolic arc of a projectile is described through past experience. It could not be described by itself as it actually happened. Consider yourself to have become instantaneously

Letters   183

conscious, (you can't because consciousness requires observation intervals processed through a complex system), riding on a projectile in the real world in the now. You would see everything in suspended animation. You surely wouldn't know where you were going because you wouldn't have the slightest idea where you had been. The differential freezes the interval and allows an instantaneous expression of compared events but those have already been observed. In your case, the past would be just as unknown on your projectile as the future. As we pass through consciously created intervals, experiencing reality in the now, however, we record our past experiences in the continuing activity of the now by our representations of them in symbolic memory. The physical world itself cannot view itself because it occurs in the instantaniety of itself and has no awareness of past or future. The differential cannot be taken in terms of the real unfolding however, for it would stop the observation as well as the observer. Since the observer "is" what it is observing, the observation interval limits the observation to certain interaction intervals.

It is the have beens that have called us to consciousness and enables us to see "causality" in the larger things of nature, and by constantly reviewing what has happened, we project ourselves beyond that moment of instantainety, in which we now exist, into the future. We were born in the now of that day. We live in the now of each day and each instant. We must look back. We must look forward. We are conscious. The unconscious essence of our nature does not look back nor forward, it unfolds in the instantainety of each now.

I have enjoyed the one way conservation. I am sure that you have probably written more than I have ever read. May the God within us bless you. Well, maybe I need to translate that so I won't be misunderstood. May the love within us be shared between us for I feel you are a man of "good deeds" from "good" seed. I hope one day you will be able to say that of me. Only in search of sweet truth.

A friend in education,
Duane Broxson

Note: This letter was sent after reading Gould's article "Four Metaphors in Three Generations" in the standing column "This View of Life". The "I am has sent us" comment in the previous letter had given him some concern. I knew it would come. This was a clarification of what I was really trying to elude to as well as an explanation for the Biblical author's intent in having used this sentence in the first place. Gould always made reference in one way or another in his articles to my comments. He knew I would recognize them and was the reason I used the phrase "one way conversation", because he never formally replied. We really were talking to each other however. I had no spell checker on the computer I was using to write most of these letters and they were written hurriedly and spontaneously. I know he was appalled at the spelling. I let this happen somewhat purposefully to create a contrast between the inspired old common country boy and the educated Harvard professor.

December 7, 1993
5882 Cedar Tree Dr.
Milton, Fl. 32570

DR. JAMES WOLFE

Dear Jimmy:

These are the last of the writings to Dr. Gould. I have never received any reply from him although I really never expected to receive one. I have wrestled with science and religion since the days of my youth. I know that many things will probably never be resolved due to the subjective nature of most of man's work. As I worked in college and read in science about geologic history and evolutionary processes, the truth they contain became very obvious to me. I was resolved to not abandon either science or religion and I have not. I have grown to appreciate both science and literature. It has been difficult though, to express ideas about these things and not be viewed as apostate by the people of my heart. Where possible, I have tried to help others understand the science of geology and evolution. You know, I am sure, that many people in my area have closed minds in regard to these subjects. I certainly have taught the principles of science as best I could without becoming overtly offensive. Since I have not participated much in the university environment, I have few persons to communicate with regarding the profound teachings of science. I read a few of Dr. Gould's articles and was impressed with his ability and style. I also sensed his profound knowledge of literature and religious philosophy. I realized he was Jewish. These are about the only things that I knew about him when I responded to one of his essays concerning what is natural and what is unnatural. In many of the articles I have read written by scientists who try to be objective, I have noted an exclusion of man and his activities from nature. It was as if, to them, what was happening with man was different from what was happening with

DUANE BROXSON. THE TEACHER

the rest of nature even though they were evolutionary biologists. I remember one occasion at the University of West Florida. We were on the lawn discussing how man was destroying the natural environment. I asked the professor what he thought about the concrete roads and highways of man. Were they natural or not? Well, these were not natural to him because man had willed these things. These were products of man's culture which was entirely different, not a part of "Raw Nature", "red in tooth and claw". This was different. Well, in view of what the principles show, I find this point of view hard to embrace and I am a Christian. It is as if man, because of his view as to what is good or bad for man, has excluded himself from it. Man is tampering with nature. It seems like to me he is as he tampers. It seems to me that he is a part of it all regardless of the outcome. As I said to Dr. Gould, if by our actions we should cause our species to become extinct, who will call it unnatural?

I felt a need to speak my view to someone with knowledge and understanding come what may. I purposefully mixed literary approaches with objectivity and I offered most of the discussions of science as a window of credibility. I am not knowledgeable in the various writings about these topics other than having a general knowledge of the chemistry of the life processes and some limited knowledge of embryology.

I remembered how our search for knowledge began together. I have always appreciated your ability.

Your friend always,
Duane Broxson

January 21, 1994
5882 Cedar Tree Dr.
Milton, Fl. 32570

DR. STEPHEN JAY GOULD,
Museum of Comparative Zoology,
Harvard University
Cambridge Mass. 02138

Dear Dr. Gould

I had decided not to say any more about what is natural or unnatural,
but in re-reading your article on metaphors, I couldn't help but reflect
on the quotation next to the Primordial Campbell's Soup can. It is
very clear here how Darwin viewed himself and man's conscious will
in relation to all of nature. Man has a tradition of viewing himself
as uniquely different from all other living creatures in that he possesses some attribute that has not been part of all other life's unfolding. Surely Christendom in Darwin's day had that tradition. Much of
that tradition remains today. Nature was viewed as the perfect creation of God. Man was viewed as God like but with fault, the sin
of his will of course. Some of this thinking, I believe, is present in
Darwin's reflections on artificial selection. "Man can act only on external and visible characters: nature cares nothing for appearances...."
"She can act...." "How fleeting are the wishes of man! How short his
time! And consequently how poor will his products be compared
with those accumulated by nature during whole geological periods."[9].
Man's wishes and efforts are set in contrast to nature which "acts on
every internal organ, on every shade of constitutional difference, on
the whole machinery of life."[10]. Man's consciousness is but one attri-

---

[9]Stephen Jay Gould, This View of Life, "Four Metaphors in Three Generations", <u>Natural History</u>,
December, 1993, pp. 20, Citing "The Origin of Species by Means of Natural Selection, 1859
[10] Ibid

188   DUANE BROXSON. THE TEACHER

bute of the whole man. Man's wishes and efforts unfolded from the same Primordial Soup Can of all life, if our evolutionary perceptions are correct. We were there during those whole geological periods, interacting, competing. We were there. We were a part and product of it all just as we are now. We have a very good idea about the length of life's past existence on earth and the length of *a* man's life, but we have little idea about the future longevity of the branch species *Homo sapiens*. That metaphorical microcosm of domestication is not the only influence that man has with his consciousness on all of the other species on this planet. Consciousness creates new avenues of interaction just as unconscious mobility did millions of years ago. As for appearances, appearances are the expression of the genotype. Selection acts on expressions of the genotype at the species level of organization and DNA of the genotype itself at the molecular level of organization. Man, with consciousness, can interact with both at the dawning of the twenty first century.

The organ that gives rise to consciousness is present in all mammals, all birds, all amphibians, all reptiles, and in all fish in such basic anatomic and physiologic similarity as to suggest a common consequence of common process. Home-box genes attest to the common consequence of much of multicellular life. If culture is possible with the human form, doesn't the possibility also manifest itself with other forms in other ways? "*Homo sapiens* was not a necessary event just a probable one."[11] Homo sapiens' competitive interaction over millions of years has established itself in relation to all other conscious living things, suppressing to some extent other forms' evolution toward a similar culture. Modern man has become the spark that caused the flame, that set the world on fire in a higher order interaction driven by the manifestation of his will to choose. When the computer was developed by man it opened the door for the possibility of complex interface networks and expanded communication impossible before its

---

[11] Stephen Jay Gould, This View of Life, "Fungal Forgery", Natural History, September, 1993 pp. 18

advent. Likewise, the thinking organ of consciousness evolved, not in just one creature but in many creatures, increasing the chance of a social, cultural evolution. Cultural man has been produced by the natural processes of nature and it is influencing, in the immediate present, the future unfolding of natural history on planet Earth. Some of the chances (however small) that will be possible in the future unfolding will be the chances that man will allow or cause to be allowed.

Yes, living things become unfit because of the actions of a conscious will. A conscious will itself could also become extinct because of its own uncontrolled actions. A species need be unfit for only a moment of geologic time to become unfit for all ages to come. The consciousness of man has reduced the effect of geologic periods to moments in some interactive respects. Billions of men engaged in the conscious war of exploitation, in selfish ambition and blind greed, are an interaction of life on earth with its own set of consequences. Selfish drive and selfish craving are obliterating ancient species by the hundreds as man expresses his conscious influence on planet Earth. Man's activity has become global and extends even into space. It was not once so. Consciousness with its match has lit this global interaction and selfishness has been its destructive aspect. It may be a blip in the great macrocosm of life, but all life is paying a high price for its selfishness. Man is creating a shift in the balances of nature by the selfish craving of the will of his collective conscious.

By what objective principle will man explain the unfolding of natural history as man himself wills this to be so and that to be so and it is so, as the God like man alters the nature of nature with his empowered hand in a sea of interaction where good can become evil, and evil can become good, where right can become wrong, and wrong can become right, in a macrocosm of persuaded subjective perception of tremendous influence? The rationality of truth can sometimes have little effect. Influence and persuasion are the tools of the subjective conscious. What other than natural selection, acting on the effects of our learned

DUANE BROXSON. THE TEACHER

experiences implemented by the precepts of our subjective interactive consciousness, can bring a working consensus to the subjective collective conscious of these masses of conscious life? "Good" cannot be zapped into the collective conscious of man. By memory of word and deed, we cry out in agony, repudiating the interactive pain of our selfish consciousness. By memory of word and deed, the exhilaration of interactive peace and harmony reinforces the spiritual vision and moral law that has inched its way into the consciousness of its masses through the hearts of "righteous" men who walked with God. Yes, it will be the selection of the effects of conscious learned experiences that man will choose to pass on to the generations by the teaching of his children in word and deed, that determines the outcome of the purposes chosen for our collective conscious. In many cases, they are as blind as the unconscious aspects of our nature. Back and forth "the good man" has rocked in contingency.[12] It is exigent that we move him to necessity.

Without considering the spiritual and moral aspects of our nature the men of science will have little effect in attempting to apply logical scientific reasoning to the monumental problems of the day. Scholars in the arts and sciences are often far advanced in their understanding of the nature of our world, but the masses of the people are not led to action by the insights of the scholars of their day, particularly the scholars of science. The destiny of a people is not so much influenced by what scholars think as by what masses of people do. What masses of people do is rooted in their political and religious culture which operates among them and by them, steeped in the handed down traditions of their ancestors. Their beliefs, which motivate their actions, become dogmatic and unchangeable almost in the light of any evidence. Gradually as human culture evolves, the great insights of the scholars of past ages find their way into the hearts and minds of the masses of the people and becomes their tradition. Human culture has

---

[12] Ibid

moved from tribal to global, and as every aspect of the evolution of biological life is still present with us, so are the various stages of our culture and the precepts that sustained them.

It is very important today for the continuation of our culture to narrow the gap between what scholars know and what the masses think. This gap has been widening rapidly in the last decades. Implementation of national solutions to the global problems of the day are important if not imperative. It will take both science and religion working together to break this "territoriality of the mind-set", this intolerance and dogmatism that threatens to thwart, or perhaps destroy altogether, the progress of human culture as we know it. If we completely remove ourselves by objective thought, we might say; "So What? The macrocosm of nature and some subdued aspect of man will probably continue." But the heartache of the billions is our own. Their hopes and dreams are our own. Their anguished cry is our own. The anguished cry of all life is our own. Will we omit man's own natural influence through our will to choose and witness the destruction and suffering of the massive billions of human kind in an anarchical hell not yet envisioned, or will man's conscious rationality join hands with the nature that produced it and alter its Malthusian course?

To deny the effects in society of the visions of our "Men of God" would be a mistake. Natural selection does not discriminate between right, wrong, truth, falsehood and deception, at the unconscious level of interaction. But through millions of years of unfolding in man, higher order consciousness, in its natural order of interaction, has brought right, wrong, truth, falsehood and deception forward into view as selection pressure mechanisms to be applied to the realm of the subjective conscious. Life now as then is a fight "between my daddy and a bad man named Hitler."[13] Selection of the effects of our higher order conscious interactions on man himself has produced this

[13] Stephen Jay Gould, This View of Life, "The Most Unkindest Cut of All", Natural History, May, 1992, pp. 4

discrimination and the will to choose, or natural bias of chance in the higher order of things, has been its father. These mechanisms involve the transmission of ideas, attitudes, and values that are favored and reinforced by man as he teaches them by word and deed to future generations. These ideas, attitudes and values also have their influence on the biological aspects of nature through the activities they allow. The Industrial Revolution, for example, has changed the nature of our interactions with living things on earth as well as our perspective of them.

Consciousness itself has begun a great feedback cycle with the nature of itself. Will it be sustained? If so, how will it be sustained? Should one rise in anger over the idiolatry of the golden calf of our self centered, materialistic culture born in the absence of the vision and morality of our spiritual law in the homes that teach the children of our land? Should we break our sacred tablets and lash out with vengeance against our own people to purge the evil from the land? Should we look for an aggressive leader of mighty men to be the champion of our will? Will the dynamics that converts the greed and selfishness of man be a man with blood on his hands or be the blood that is shed by innocent man? Can love grow where the blood fell and make the tabernacle of all nature the heart of man? In either case, the inheritance of the "genes" of learned experiences will be tested by the competitive interaction of our collective conscious, by the interaction of man with all other life, and by the effect of the dynamic state of our physical world and be found favorable or unfavorable.

With all of the power and strength of my deepest honor, I can here myself cry; "General Lee, to the rear! General Lee, to the rear![14] And on the strength of that honor, I feel I would have charged forward and with my own hand attempted to purge my evil brother from the land. But he was not my evil brother , or was I there evil brother, and they

[14] Willard Webb, ed., Crucial Moments of the Civil War, (New York: Bonanza Books, 1959) p. 276

knew that of themselves. It was the "territoriality of the mind-set", steeped in tradition and honor, amplifying the aggressive competitive nature of the human male, that caused both brothers to compete to the death at that moment in space and time. It has been the aggressive selfish behavior of the human male that has caused much of the agony suffered by mankind throughout the record of our written history. Much of our learned tradition has been the father of our hatred. More than any day, we must press forward to remove this territoriality of the mind-set, this pervasive, socially inherited, destructive aspect that pits North against South, Black against White, Christian against Muslim, Arab against Jew. It cannot happen over night, or without further conflict, but it can happen. History has shown us, we will not be zapped by a supernatural God. It must, if it does, unfold within the heart of mankind. It can happen through world wide communication and interaction with good will. It can happen through the reinforcement in our society of the "better angels of our nature"[15] but to be implemented, it must be taught by word and deed in the communities and homes of the children of the world. We program our offspring with the "genes" of our own learned experiences. We must replace this destructive aspect of man's nature with new visions that embrace a common hope for all men. We must strive to make the visions of our ancestors, who were willing to challenge the tradition of their day to bring a blessing to all mankind, our vision. We must go out to Samaria. Whites must learn to love Blacks and Blacks Whites. Christians must learn to love Muslims and Muslims Christians. Arabs must learn to love Jews and Jews Arabs. But not just love them, love them enough to destroy the traditions that are the wedges that divide them. If Christians could only see past the intolerant, dogmatic doctrine that has arisen from the spirit of the Masterful Servant, we might grasp this —

deepest sense of a truly universal community- the equal

---

[15] Stephen Jay Gould, This View of Life, "The Most Unkindest Cut of All", Natural History, May, 1992, pp. 11, Citing Abraham Lincoln's First Inaugural Address, March, 1861

worth of all as explressions of a single entity, the species
Homo sapiens, whatever our individual misfortunes or
disabilities-then Isaiah's vision could be realized, and our
human wolves would dwell in peace with lambs,---[16]

What Christian will carry this cross? What Muslim can break the dogmatic bonds of Islam that generate so much hatred and intoler-ance? What Jew can break the dogmatic bonds of Judaism and reach out his hand to both Arab and Christian and make them one in spirit as they are one in God? Is Jerusalem really a test for mankind?

I am sure that many wars will rage in the future history of man. Many souls will cry to the heavens for relief of their anguish. The selfish stupidity, heartache and agony of Somalia and Sarajevo cries aloud to the memory of our conscious this very day. But hopefully that rem-nant of struggling souls, "when they are touched as surely they will be"[17] , will continue to carry the visions of a nobler man ever onward until he embraces the old vision of a New Jerusalem where no "evil" shall enter. What grander vision could enlightened man have, con-sidering the conscious hell that has unfolded on this planet Earth for the eater and the eaten, the killer and the killed, for the powerless and impoverished but conscious masses? Will the blood and suffering of innocence, crying out in our own hearts, implement our visions for the hope of our people by modifying the competitive interaction of our collective conscious? Will our children and our children's chil-dren be blessed by the actions we take?

Our part in this unfolding will be over shortly. If for some people, it appears only as words, let it be the words for the words sake. What future it holds, will be seen by others. Will other similar forms crafted by our grand mother chance, over millions of years, observe and re-

---

[16] Stephen Jay Gould, This View of Life, "The Most Unkindest Cut of All", Natural History, May, 1992, pp. 11
[17] Gould, "The Most Unkindest Cut of All", pp. 11, Citing Abraham Lincoln's First Inaugural Address

flect upon the power of our own interactions? Can our grand mother chance be fathered by the spirit of our visions and change forever the future unfolding of our nature? Is there a universal good far beyond the powers of our immediate observation that will reject us if we fail? Will our visions be sustained in the vast reaches of space by form and power unknown and spirit yet unseen? As for me, I will dream of spirit yet unseen.

We are tempted by the conscious realization of the power of our will to cause destruction and heartache for our own selfish reasons. But we have interfaced our own personal consciousness with those of our fellow man, and to some extent, with our fellow species. And when in agony and despair we cry out for ourselves, we also cry out in empathy for all men and all other life. When our hearts fill with joy and happiness and our spirit is lifted by the winds to the mountain top of personal experience, we also carry the joy and happiness of all men and all other life. With the power of our minds we stand at the door and look, not only for ourselves but because of ourselves, for all our brothers and for all other life, for we have the conscious power to affect all life. We must have visions of a higher mountain as those of old. We must stamp with our feet and find the spiritual water of our dried up watering hole, for all conscious nature thirsts.

> *Is not this the fast that I have chosen? To loose the bands of wickedness, to undo the heavy burdens, and to let the oppressed go free, and that ye break every yoke? Is it not to deal thy bread to the hungry, and that thou bring the poor that are cast out to thy house? When thou seest the naked, that thou coverest him: and that thou hide not thyself from thine own flesh? Then shall thy light break forth as the morning---*[18]

---

[18] Holy Bible, Isaiah 58: 7-8

DUANE BROXSON. THE TEACHER

"Behold my servant, whom I uphold; mine elect, in whom my soul delighteth; I have put my spirit upon him:"[19]

From the days of his youth the Masterful Servant looked back. He looked back at the stories and tales associated with the advent of his birth. He looked deep into the heart of his mother. He looked deep into the history and spirituality of his own people. He looked deep into the manifestation of evil in his own age. He looked upon the miserable state of much of the humanity that surrounded him. He looked back at the vision of Isaiah. The voice of Isaiah crying out, touched his heart and the depths of his inner soul. Amid the conquest of wars, destruction, and lamentation for the souls of his people, he saw the light of spiritual victory. He looked at the manifestation of power in his own mind. He returned from the wilderness of deep introspection; from a battle with evil in his own consciousness. He embraced with all of the spirit of his being, for all men, the vision of Isaiah, deeply understanding its purpose and outcome.

> *The spirit of the Lord is upon me, because he hath anointed me to preach the Gospel to the poor: he hath sent me to heal the broken hearted, to preach deliverance to the captives, and recovery of sight to the blind, to set at liberty them that are bursed—*
> *And he began to say unto them, This day is this scripture fulfilled in your ears.*[20]

From that moment on, He looked forward. He became Isaiah's purpose maker. From that moment on, He became the incarnation of the vision of Isaiah by his own choice. He became the Servant of his Spiritual Father.

Isaiah's vision still lives. The Masterful Servant's vision still lives. It

---

[19] Holy Bible, Isaiah 42:1
[20] Holy Bible, Luke 4:18-21

condemns the war lords of Somalia through the starvation of its naked masses. It condemns the malicious hatred of Sarajevo through the cries of its suffering innocent as it did Auschvitz. It condemns the malicious hatred of Gaza through the weeping and wailing of the heartbroken Arab and Jewish mothers. He weeps again at the sepulcher of their Holy Fathers. His voice still echos off their Holy Mountain. It still rings like a resonating bell through the hearts of mankind. It is a vision for all ages and all men, as it was in the beginning just north of Ur, "great mountain, country of the universe, filled with enduring light."[21]

Yours truly,
Duane Broxson

* A copy of "The Insight of the Masses Bless Your hearts" was included.

---

[21] Samuel Noah Kramer, "The World of Abraham", Everyday life in Bible Times," A Volume in the Story of Man Library, National Geographic Society, 1967, pp. 54, Citing Clay Tablet of Sumer.

DUANE BROXSON. THE TEACHER

February 2, 1994
5882 Cedar Tree Dr.
Milton, Fl. 32570

DR. STEPHEN JAY GOULD,
Museum of Comparative Zoology,
Harvard University
Cambridge, Mass. 02138

Dear Dr. Gould:

In reference to your article, "The Persistently Flat Earth", I would like to re-word for you the first discourse of the preacher in "The Insight of the Masses Bless Their Hearts". I have no way of knowing for sure that you have even read this discourse, but I wanted to assure you that such sentiment is very present in the Bible Belt of the Southeastern United States.

> *Anyone with any common sense should know that all life was created just as it is now by the Devine Creator in the very beginning. Why, these pseudo-intellectuals, all caught up in their theories of evolution are just corrupting the minds of our children. We should burn the universities, if that's all they can teach our children, and send these fellows off to the funny farm where they belong.*

I wouldn't go so far as to say they would burn the universities, but they give university professors of evolution very little credibility. I can assure you that the enlightened scholars of theology also have the same credibility difficulty here in the Southeast. I was not really thinking how scholars of science and scholars of theology relate in thought to one another.

The evolution in thought of the shape of the earth, so far as I knew, began with the thinking of the Greeks and Eratosthenes. I had always taught in science that the shape of the earth was well established by scholars at the time of Columbus. I used the obvious fallacy of the flat earth as a point to emphasize a more subtle point in the second dialogue of the teacher. My message to the people of my heart is that their views of the immutability of the species are about as credible today as that of a flat earth. Also, it relates the difficulty with which the insights of science become common knowledge and the sacrifices that are made by those who are responsible for great shifts in the perspective of the common man. We both know that science is dynamic in its nature, questioning its own precepts, and constantly adjusting itself based on the credibility of its investigations. Religion, however is not dynamic. It is static and is based on accepted absolutes. It takes considerable time for changes to take place in the precepts held by large groups of its people. Take for example, the absolute literal interpretation of Biblical Scripture by very conservative Christians in the Southeast. Religious thought of the common man today is in a period of adjustment due largely to the explosion of scientific knowledge and insight. Any significant adjustment in religious thought is a very painful process for its followers. My work is a plea for new insights in religious thought, particularly Christian thought. It is also a plea for the cooperation of science and religion. The significant insights of both, as they apply to the needs of the day, are in desperate need of implementation.

Both science and religion suffer from dogmatic tradition as you have said. Science recovers quickly because change is programmed into the scientific process and because science is somewhat international and has no overall connection to biological and territorial ancestry. The religious thoughts of the masses are tied strongly to their social, biological and territorial ancestry which acts as a buffer against appropriate change.

There are basic underlying concepts that describe rationality, but what is irrational today from one point of view, can become highly rational tomorrow from another view, and vice versa. Science can attest to this.

It is the human mind that is the father of both science and religion. Both are searching. Both are a natural unfolding of a natural mind however unique. One day, perhaps, on their different journeys, they shall find each other.

Yours truly,
Duane L. Broxson

March 7, 1994
5882 Cedar Tree Dr.
Milton, Fl. 32570

JAMES L. WOLFE,
3600 Michele Ct.
Mobile, Ala. 36605

Dear Jimmy:

I received your letter of last year. In my last letter, I mentioned that those were the last writings to Dr. Gould. I have, however, sent him these last two articles which you will find inclosed. I believe I sent you a copy of "The insight of the Masses Bless Their Hearts". One of these articles expresses the intent of that writing. The other speaks about how the evolution of our consciousness and will is obviously connected to the natural selection and evolution of all other life over the ages. I have applied the same thinking in regard to conscious thought and the transmission of ideas and values. These ideas are briefly mentioned in the other writings. All life seems to be based on structural and process memory as outlined in the first paper, "Some Ideas Worth and Not Worth Reading". The second writing, "On the Evolution of Choice", shows how evolved choice is basic to the interction of all life and also involves memory of experiences in the natural interaction of life processes with each other and the physical environment.

Natural selection stabalizes, shapes, and forms the unfolding of unconscious memory in structure and form in the evolution of organisms from a biochemical point of view. After a man passes on his genes to his offspring his contribution to the gene pool is over. His activity as a selection pressure mechanism, however is not over. I can see this same activity taking place in the realm of the subjective conscious in the transmission of the ideas and values of our learned experiences. The brain is plastic. That is, it can be programmed. When any program or memory is recorded into the mind an actual physical imprinting in structure and process takes place. We know these are not passed on by the chemical genes of our inheritance unless they somehow internally influence the sexual genome of the individual. I won't think on that possibility now. However, our ideas and values are taught by word and deed to our offspring. They are imprinted into the minds and hearts of our offspring. I have called the vehicle for the transmission of these ideas and values into the minds of our offspring the "genes" of learned experiences. They are acquired characteristics but they can be passed on to future generations. In the masses they overlap generations of biological offspring. The dynamic interaction of these ideas, values and etc. produce selection pressures that either favor their retention and transmission or do not. They become selected by their own processes of interaction as are our biological interactions. I have mentioned how I think some of these are retained and passed on and the dynamics that is involved. Our ideas and values evolve within the realm of the subjective conscious and become a part of an overall collective conscious. Consciousness in humans has led to purpose. We have become by our own evolution purpose makers. We can with intent change the nature of our interactions.

What is time to an unconscious physical phenomenon? Does it look back? Does it look forward? Shucks, it doesn't look at all. It just unfolds in the instantaniety of the moment. My question of time is not beyond the realm of possibility. Think about it. All consciousness is based on memory of past experiences retained in symbolic form in structure and function that continues to interact in the now. Perceived time based on interactions is a conscious activity. With it we compare events within the system by the system itself as it (the system) unfolds in the biological and physical aspects of our consciousness. Throw in simultaneity for all events just to promote some thinking on the matter. We know we can't observe events simultaneously. Whether or not a physical process is occurring at a faster rate in one system or the other, or whether basic aspects of the system are changing, does not preclude an over all simultaniety of events however unobservable. If events are occurring simultaneously, perceived time doesn't exist within the system itself until historical comparisons of intervals are made. Comparisons of intervals cannot be made in the now unless symbolic recall of events takes place. The conscious mind does retain in symbolic memory a history of events that unfold. It is with this historic memory that the conscious mind perceives time. Our objective view is based on symbolic representations of events and not the events themselves. Biological life itself is based on historic memory as cyclic phenomenon bring similar events into interaction, however this memory is an unconscious one. Think about it. There is no *life* of the past. There is no life occurring before it occurs. There is a memory of the past, written in the symbolic memory of our minds and books as well as in Earth's geologic record that are also existing in the now. With our consciousness we of course realize the occurrence of events but our essence is at the same instant part of the unfolding events as they occur. There is no real rational evidence that these same events occur again. The evidence is quite the contrary. Dr Gould has mentioned the huge probability against the re-occurring of complex events in another unfolding of biological evolution. What is the probability of the same events unfolding? Your guess is as good as mine. Quantum physicists contemplate some of these questions. They also discuss many dimensions. The real question here is how close the logically deduced symbolic representations of reality we have formulated in memory can come to actual reality as it unfolds. We project using memory and causality into the future. Our conscious view of the universe expands as the memory of our experiences expands. We expand our experiences with our own intent. Science is an activity of this nature. We look back into the recorded history of past events to decipher relationships to the unfolding now and record, as we ourselves proceed on in the process, the outcome which we also categorize in memory as conclusions to be again applied. We retain the symbolic record of our memories and past experiences with our books, records, disks, tapes and etc. Our logic and relationships are expressed in our equations of mathematics. We teach them to the generations. They evolve as aspects of our culture. Our own physical and chemical processes are recorded in the DNA of our genes, programmable cell membrane memory, physiological memory pathways and chemical memory pathways that I have mentioned before.

In what I have written, I have not included credits because I have not formally researched these ideas. I have written all of this material from contemplation drawing on the knowledge I have of physical and chemical systems. A little generality won't hurt, I don't think, in a sea of specific and specialized hypothesizing. I know that the thinking of others influences all of us. These are just ideas for what they are worth, if anything. I hope they haven't been a waste of your time. I know you are a busy person.

I have four to five preparations to make for classes each year and I also work weekends in the laboratory at Sacred Heart Hospital. With the responsibilities of a family and young children, my time is spread thin.

I would be interested in references to any work that you have done to see where and how your are thinking on matters.

Your friend,
Duane Broxson

March 20, 1994
5882 Cedar Tree Dr.
Milton, Fl 32570

DR. BERNID HEINRICH,
Zoology Department
University of Vermont,
Burlington, Vermont

I enjoyed reading your article on what is natural. I have also read other articles that you have written. The one on the Raven was interesting indeed. I was a bit disappointed though, to read that "Biological reality has nothing to say about morality, because natural is what is nothing more." That natural is what is and nothing more is a point I have been trying to make lately, but taken from a different view of biological reality.

In your article you said: "Our limited biological morality-which may be partially encoded in genes- concerns rules and behavior relative to our immediate fellow humans. It is natural for us because we are social."... "Our natural morality once sufficed to keep us moral." In this age of bacteria our consciousness has allowed us to make the connection between bacteria and man but the dichotomies just keep coming: living and nonliving, plant and animal, unconscious and conscious, good and evil. I agree: "The biggest reality of the world is neither of conjecture, belief nor moral conviction. It is one of incomparable practical urgency. It is one that requires our attention because it affects all of life acutely." Acting on that practical urgency in an attempt to affect a solution will not come about without engaging the conjecture, belief and moral conviction that do abound in our societies. Again you say: "Natural laws are not made by authority. Instead they are descriptions of how individuals actually do behave when they are given the freedom to act." The conceptualization of morality

DUANE BROXSON. THE TEACHER

has come about as the result of this very natural process. I understand your distinction when you say: "Now by having another baby we are in no small way affecting in the long term the whole globe, and all of life on it.".... "Such linkage is a new fact of present reality, and the choices we need to make are not just "natural" biological choices. They are moral ones.", but I respectfully disagree with the "natural" part of it, as if moral choices were not natural. For to me, life is a continuum from the nonliving to the living, from the plant to the animal, from unconsciousness to consciousness, from instinct to purpose and not a dichotomy. I see them as a natural part of the unfolding of life even if we are a tidbit offshoot of our total grand evolutionary view. I see the religious aspect of the consciousness of man as a natural interaction of man, unfolding with his consciousness (right or wrong, true or false, fact or fiction) along with all the other social behavior that man has engaged. It has surely had its influence in our small human realm. Our small tidbit of a human realm is surely putting the selection pressure on many a living thing at this point in time. I feel like you, that the men of science should engage the moral issues for the moral issues of man affect all life. It is this very fact that should make them clearly natural. For, as you say, what is a law of nature? The activities of the molecules have brought into view the "laws" through which we express our desired interactive experiences and we do not desire without experience. The genes have their part. The higher order interactions have their part. They both interact together. *E. coli* can make insulin now.

As we anticipate the future and the possible scenarios that unfold before our minds and computer screens, we realize that only the power of a united purpose can change the Malthusian outcome of such tragedies as we can envision unfolding before us. Such outcomes have always been natural, but consciousness has made them tragedies in view of our own kind and in some enlightened respects those of other species. Diversion of such a tragedy, if we can make it so, will also be natural.

It is beyond me why evolutionary biologists have such trouble bridging the gap between instinctive and unconscious interaction and interaction controlled to some extent by learning, will and purpose in regard to what is natural. Do we limit what is natural to Darwin's conceptualization of interactive biology which, by the notion of artificial selection alone, seemed to separate man's will from what is natural. Or do we include all possibilities, however remote and unique, that nature has allowed to unfold within the life process? One of the greatest insights of the twentieth century, I believe, is the conformation scientifically of man's oneness with all of the biological and physical aspects of the world around us. My God! A tree is my brother! I have not brought this into view. The men of science like yourselves in all of the sciences have brought this to view. A oneness that was interactively known to early man, but was conceptually lost to many, especially since the industrial revolution.

Darwin's mechanism of natural selection gave us the tool to understand and substantiate much of the evolutionary processes of life. It has allowed us to see that nature, though consistent in the manifestation of its physical form, is not static but is divergent in its continuing interaction. Nature constantly changes her interactive aspects. The idea of evolution can be applied to almost any interactive level because it simply says that the interactions of organisms among themselves and with all of the other factors in the environment has determined and will determine the interactive behavior that will be allowed to continue by whatever mechanism. Evolution is more comprehensive that survival of the fittest in the sense of "red in tooth and claw". What difference does it make whether the interactions are conscious or unconscious, blind or chosen by a will or a purpose? In the natural sense, the interactions they produce help fashion the outcome.

Choices of behavior made under the influence of moral pressure are choices which affect the interactions of man and whose influence in-

DUANE BROXSON. THE TEACHER

directly extends to many other living things. They are just as natural as any other choice of action or responsiveness that precipitates any other interaction, for interaction is the very essence of nature herself. What is a moral idea in the mind? Can I just make a moral proclamation and cause it to become "law"? Morality, of whatever nature, has unfolded with us manifested in the interactions that, over the ages, have caused them to come into conscious view. They exist among us as interactions, that by our own activity we can influence, but not totally formulate. Morality did not first exist in the abstraction of our minds. Morality began in our unfolding interactions that formed from all our experiences throughout the vague depths of lower level consciousness and instinct of the past to the higher order interactions of the now in its various settings. In fact, if it exists only in the symbolic nature of our minds, or only on the pages of a Hebraic text it has no significant consequence. It must be expressed as an interactive behavior. When it is expressed as an interactive behavior it is natural for all nature is an interaction. They were not first abstract concepts formulated by great thinkers and forced upon a people even if it sometimes appears so. Human morality resulted from the gradual unfolding of interactions between men as a reality among themselves to be iterated, formulated and manifested formally in the symbolic mind by great thinkers and leaders primarily as a tool for instruction and teaching which was never divorced from the importance of practice. In their various settings man's learned experiences overlap generations, being passed on by both word and deed. Word being a symbolic form of a more important deed. Man's consciousness and symbolic memory did not unfold overnight. We tend to overlook the fact that man's consciousness has gradually come on line over the eons of time, for we had to organically evolve the thinking organ and all of the interactions that came about as a result of it, as did all other living things that possess it. We evolved it historically as a species and we evolve it out of our history and modify it to our present setting as we pass from zygote to adulthood in its present settings. Just ask any Gaza Palestinian or Jericho Jew. Great moral leaders have

Letters   209

amplified what they have deduced and then hoped for, from their own natural experience.

Man has evolved a higher order interaction which allows him, in that arena, to choose his responses and actions. It is when his personal experience becomes interfaced with members of his own kind and when his own personal experiences can be viewed as influencing the feedback behavior of others, that he begins iterating behaviors that we call moral. Our morality has always been in view of others and what they perceive of us. We know that individuals are biologically unique in many respects and respond to interactions differently. We have a distribution of interactive behavior in terms of our own codified, well established moral "laws". This has been obvious even though some of them have been written in stone.

Yes, I would say man's visions are natural. We formulate the higher order interactions in our minds through our collective experiences and as we globally integrate our experiences, we each cry for each other and we each laugh for each other. And as this great human consciousness unfolds our own experiences formulate the "rules" of our behavior that become "beautiful and good" for us. Surely we have realized that what is good and beautiful for us also depends upon our interaction with all other life.

We see our inner selves as we have seen our origins, frightening and deep, possessing the potential for choices that may bring heartache or joy. We have interfaced ourselves in consciousness with our brothers and in the joining of our hands, rang the death knell for some of the pleasure of our own selfish consciousness. We must search for the "better angles of our nature" for all life, because we have the power to affect all life. Whatever we do, in my opinion, will be natural, for life to me is an unfolding and all of its interactions are natural.

Gone is our view of an exalted man and a separate and special creation. After all, what is man that nature should be mindful of him save in his own interactive consciousness? Looming before us are our choices and their consequences. Most important are the choices that affect our children and our children's children. "Train up a child in the way he should go and when he is old he will not depart from it." A wise proverb of Solomon, lacking no less in wisdom at the dawning of the twenty first century. What is lacking is a sound and fairly universal view of the way they should go. Could it be that one day our will and purpose will allow us to train up our children not only as South Africans, or as Americans, or as Russians, or as Bosnians, or as Serbs, or as Palestinians, or as Israeli but as brothers? Brothers with differences of course, but fellow *Homo sapiens*. And not just fellow *Homo sapiens*, but sharers of the great bio-diversity of planet Earth through which flows the essence of our natural heat beat.

Your friend in Education,
Duane L. Broxson

May 23, 1994
Central High School
Milton, Fl. 32570

DR. BERND HEINRICH,
Zoology Dept.
University of Vermont,
Burlington, Vermont

Dear Dr. Heinrich:

I have included a couple of my ideas: "Pretty Little Flower by the Field Fence Line" and "Tis the Raven Nothing More". I thought you might be interested in reading them. The raven poem was written before I read your article on the raven in Natural History Magazine. This idea of natural has been with me for some time but I have never tried to express myself about it until recently. It was not hard for me to extend what I had learned about evolution to our own view of ourselves.

Human social behavior is very complex and intriguing. Though some scientists would only include the physical biochemical aspects of our biology as natural, they are defiantly interconnected and interact with man's conscious activity and social behavior. A bird can sit on the fence and plant trees but the fence is unnatural? It is hard to not see ourselves as we see ourselves! Oops!

Yours respectively,
Duane Broxson

DUANE BROXSON. THE TEACHER

August 11, 1994
5882 Cedar Tree Dr.
Milton, Fl. 32570

TIME MAGAZINE LETTERS,
Time & Life Building-Rockefeller Center,
New York, New York 10020

Dear Editor:

RE: Our Cheating Hearts

Mr. Wright says: "We are potentially moral animals-which is more
than any other animal can say-but we are not naturally moral animals." If by subjecting ourselves to moral scrutiny we become fully
moral, will the order we created by our purpose and intent no longer
be natural? Will we have separated ourselves from nature and be unnatural? It seems that some of our evolutionary thought is still stuck
in an old tradition. When in the course of our evolutionary history did
our will become unnatural scientifically speaking? It is really more
like Forest Gump in all respects. Natural (that is, what we perceive to
exist including ourselves) is as natural does.

Respectfully yours,
Duane Leonidas Broxson
904-623-4969

August 10, 1994
Central High School
Milton, Fl. 32570

JACK RUDLOE,
Gulf Specimens Marine Laboratories Inc.
P.O. Box 237,
Panacea, Florida 32346

Dear Jack:

I didn't forget about the brief discussion we had about the effect of computer technology on our creative grasp of the real world. The article I mentioned is inclosed.

I have done a little writing of my own over the years. Most of it in the area of creative literature of a short nature. I have had many ideas about science that I never tried to express in written form. One of these ideas came about as a result of my struggle with my own religious heritage and science as I studied evolutionary theory in college. I realized quickly the credibility of the profound precepts of evolutionary theory. They challenged many of the doctrinal issues of the faith of my youth. I realized that I had a difficult matter to deal with. I decided early on to pursue both of these interests, realizing the contribution that each of them had made on the unfolding of man down through the ages. I would not abandon either for both had produced a significant influence. I really gave this some serious thought. Thought that has lasted a lifetime. When I embrace something, it is not done lightly. If we evolved from the primordial chemical soup, so to speak, then every aspect of man's nature was natural. This had to include his conscious will and purpose. Creation, what we perceive to exist, is the real father of the consciousness that we possess. I puzzled over this obvious connection. Through the years I would read mate-

DUANE BROXSON. THE TEACHER

rial written by evolutionary biologists that always seemed to exclude what man did with his will and purpose from nature. His fences were unnatural. His highways were unnatural. His buildings were unnatural. It is a very common perspective, but for the life of me, I could not understand it. Here were the very men that had revealed a much distressing fact to me, limiting their own conceptual scheme when it came to man's will and purpose because of their own bias. I don't mean here to condone by default everything that man has done, but just to emphasize that everything man does will have its own natural consequence as nature unfolds either conscious or unconscious. We cannot exclude ourselves from it just because we recognize our own creative impact upon it, because we are it (nature that is). We are both creation and consciousness. If consciousness takes us beyond the limited perception we now have of natural selection, that too will be natural.

Well, I did finally respond with some expressions of my own. The insight that I was able to realize though, was that religious precepts could really be real! That is, they had influence on the natural unfolding of things whether they were true or false. Truth, falsehood or deception does not prohibit the influence an interaction has on other interactions. Some kind of influence will occur. Interactions are the essence of nature herself. The interplay of interactions has shaped the nature we know from the first life to now. The conscious mind has brought truth, falsehood and deception into view as selection pressure mechanisms acting on the realm of the *subjective conscious*. That is, the behaviors or interactions that the conscious mind as a collective body will allow to be acquired and expressed through interacting, teaching and learning. The conscious mind is plastic and can acquire characteristics. Some of these characteristics involve interactive behavior. Interactive behavior will be tested by all aspects of the world in which it occurs and be found favorable or unfavorable. Our choices become evolved choices and the behaviors that result become evolved behaviors. The conscious mind's activity overlaps generations giving it continuity. It has brought morality and ethics into view in our own complex realms of social interaction through the selection of its own evolved choices. Religious thinking evolved from the interactive experiences of all those involved. I was excited when I read Robert Wright in the August issue of Time Magazines, "Our Cheating Hearts", say:

"It massively wastes the most precious evolutionary resource: love." Religion and science at last! I thought! But I was dumbfounded again when I read:

> *Darwin himself believed the human species to be a moral one- in fact, the only moral species. "A moral being is one who is capable of comparing his past and future actions or motives, and of approving or disapproving of them," he wrote. In this sense, yes, we are moral. We have at least the technical capacity to lead an examined life: Self-awareness, memory, foresight and judgment. Still, chronically subjecting ourselves to moral scrutiny and adjusting our behavior accordingly is hardly a reflex. We are potentially moral animals-which is more than any other animal can say-but we are not naturally moral animals. (Italics mine) The first step to being moral is to realize how throughly we aren't."*

Tell me how anything can be an evolutionary resource and not be natural. He says when we start engaging in moral behavior this is not part of the naturally unfolding part of life on the earth. It has somehow become separated from it. I guess it has become supernatural.

In view of the above lengthy comment, I have included a reply I made to an article appearing in Discovery Magazine. I thought you might like to read it.

Thanks for your time. I hope to bring my two boys down to view your specimens, possibly next summer. They would enjoy that.

Yours truly,
Duane Broxson

March 15, 1995
5882 Cedar Tree Dr.
Milton, Fl. 32570

DR. STEPHEN JAY GOULD,
Museum of Comparative Zoology,
Harvard University
Cambridge, Mass. 02138

It is fascinating to contemplate the realization of an outcome, out of all the possible outcomes, as the single view of progress we can have, from an evolutionary view point. It is also fascinating to see how those outcomes reflect aspects of a synchronated symphony of wholeness, which seems to be more, in truth, than a part of it can imagine.

Any view of life displays the many and varied faces that it has so clearly presented. All organisms have existed continuously over recollections in history, as progressions, (not in the cultural sense), creating the great diversity of differences we see in their larger structures. Even the single cell bacterium is a progression in the time frame of our minds. One event after the other occurred as it maintained its life processes in its journey through space and time. As we see them, the progressions have been molded by all events coming to bear upon them, (whether chance or otherwise), flowing over the eons of now, which have become our pages of recollected history. And we have seen them most of the time as single lines rather than the integrated one that some are beginning to imagine them to be. We have tended to view these as linear progressions, omitting in our memories their constant interconnected wholeness and relatedness both laterally and progressively, which even now is difficult to fathom and comprehend. Has it not been a divergent progression toward complexity for some, that led to the conscious comprehension of some aspects of itself? Not that we were destined to have become ourselves, but that we *have*

DUANE BROXSON. THE TEACHER

become ourselves; that chance in the natural order of things has fashioned a will that can, with intent, feed back into the nature of itself. One occurring in the interrelatedness of its wholeness, and not apart from it.

We evolved amid all of this interconnected wholeness by the natural "laws" that we have reckoned as causality in our symbolic replay of history. What are the laws of nature but all of the things that did happen played in an arena of all the possible things that could happen, with the complete scope of the could happen unknown, and the did happen only partially known? Out of this have come ourselves, the watchers. But we are more than watchers. We are discerners of part of the could happen and choosers of part of the will happen and this touches every aspect of the whole as we interact within its wholeness. We ourselves have become in will what we always were, law makers by chance or otherwise in the grand unfolding.

I can here now, after the outpouring of his questioning soul over the fate of his people, the unfolding vision of Habakkuk:

> And the Lord answered me, and said, Write the vision, and
> make it plain upon tables, that he may run that readeth it.
> For the vision is yet for an appointed time, but at the end it
> shall speak and not lie: Though it tarry, wait for it: because it
> will surely come, it will not tarry.
> Behold, his soul which is lifted up is not upright in him: but
> the just shall live by faith.

It has become more and more evident; this Lord is not a supernatural Lord unaccustomed to the whims of chance, but a natural chooser of the choices brought into view before him, unfolding in his own evolution, in his own tabernacle, for this moment, and for the visions of his tomorrow. (Please excuse the personal pronouns. View it as a "collapse of the wave function".)

So it is the progressive diversity, reflecting every moment and detail of its existence in its fit with the now, that bewilders us, and is the beauty of this way of life. No Sir, I cannot imagine a "Hot Headed, Naked, Ice Borer" on Noah's Ark, but I can imagine the unfolding of a mind or minds fashioning the underlying principles of a righteous Noah from the heartbreaks and joys of their experiences. I can imagine the evolution of a higher order fit unfolding with will through the pages of our recollected history.

The idea of age exists in our memories and in our perceptions. It has moved, as you have said, together, all entwined with each other through the countless ages of our ability to reconstruct a memory either in history through our analysis of our physical world, or in the now of our own mental processes. But truly, it exists only now. How long is a now? Now is forever. Forever is open-ended.

An innate interaction must observe an interval, as I have said, in order to bring itself to consciousness. It is the *cognizance* of a *symbolic* interval that becomes time and gives us our will. For an innate system with chance as its father, I would be tempted to call this "progress" whether it becomes dead ended or not! The system itself, utilizes itself to construct an interpretation of itself.

We shouldn't get so concerned about differences between races or individuals' unique abilities. We should get concerned, however, when abilities are equated with worth. The writers of the Declaration of Independence did not assert that all people were created equal in ability or physical characteristics, the disparity of which they themselves were examples, but they did assert the equal worth of individuals in their sight. This idea of equal worth translates into equal rights for those who are responsible and abide by the principles themselves. All men do not embrace this quality of equal worth, either because of one's inability to demonstrate, in their actions, the principles that created this view, or because of their own biases and differences of opinion. It is our inheritance that motivates us to associate worth with ability and certain physical characteristics. This is the way it has been in our struggle to survive on this earth. This is the way it seems to be in a system of rewards through free enterprise, if it becomes excessively exploitative or abusive.

When the worth of individuals diminish, so do their rights. This ideal of equal worth requires feed back from a collective consciousness and cannot be sustained amid the overwhelming expression of certain behaviors. The acceptance of proper behavior, in this view, cannot be dictated by formal "laws" that do not have their roots in a collectively shared experience.

We must extend this idea of worth even beyond the limits of our own species. It can come only in the framework of our future interactions, after enough feedback has accumulated to fill the heartbeat of a collective conscious.

The teaching of Christianity does not assert the equal abilities of all people, but rather their uniqueness. For some, it does assert the equal worth of all people regardless of their station in life. (Some Christians view of this is their equal unworthiness.) It also places the test of this in ones ability to demonstrate these principles in real experience.

The worth of the individual is the part of the value system that has made America great in the enactment of the Declaration of Independence. The Declaration of Independence, and the ideas that proceeded from it, was a vision of how human relations could be, as viewed from experience. It was the embracing of these ideas in actual practical experience that enacted the grand vision. The vision stimulates and motivates the particular experiences which through expression become the realization of the vision.

Ever so does some aspects of our human relations evolve becoming part of our traditions passed on in memory through learned experiences. As much as we would like, however, we cannot separate the interaction of learned and unlearned conscious and unconscious behavior from the existence we now cogitate and enjoy because it really is an interconnected whole.

The experiment of our own will will continue. We may botch and bungle but we do will. Has this not always been the case? What is the test of any interactive behavior but the consequence of its own interaction? We did not decide that we would will. This came about through the very processes we are trying to describe. This is the exciting aspect of it. The innate and unlearned experience is the father of our will, either viewed embryologically or phylogenetically into history. The life system has begun to feedback with its will as it has with all of its innate cyclic phenomenon. Feedback with will is a puzzlement even to ourselves. So much so, we dare to call it progress. But it can just as easily be motivated by one vision as it can another. Such was the case with the underlying vision propelling the Allied and Axis powers. But feedback comes through our experiences!

> *For the stone shall cry out of the wall, and the beam out of the timber shall answer it. Woe to him that buildeth a town with blood, and stablisheth a city by iniquity!*

I can still see Eisenhower on the field of the dead reminding us. I can still see it in the memory of all I hold dear. I can here Isaiah also crying out a hope for the hearts of his people! Crying out a hope even now through our memories of righteousness for all people!

> *For as the rain cometh down, and the snow from heaven, and return not thither, but watereth the earth, and maketh it bring forth and bud, that it may give seed to the sower, and bread to the eater: So shall my word be that goeth forth out of my mouth: it shall not return unto me void, but it shall*

accomplish that which I please, and it shall prosper in the thing whereto I sent it.

On this earth the works of "God" in the human realm are performed by human hands that are motivated by human hearts. In other words, "God" is an attempt to conceptualize in another way the working essence of the physical system that science is trying so hard to describe, and that physical system is also ourselves in experience, the participators and the describers. Not only is he the creator but he is also the creation. Part of this is made known by the attitudes and values attested to and evaluated by the system itself. It is through the enactment of these attitudes and values found in the minds of men and the effects they have on behavior that expresses the concept of God within. This was a teaching of Jesus the Master Servant.

A false icon? Are not all of our icons false in some respect, reflecting as you say, our own innermost prejudice? The Ptolemaic view was a false icon that led to our perception of the Copernican system. Each functioning in its own right. The planetary model of the atom was in part a false icon, yet it became a platform from which to launch new, more comprehensive and fascinating views of our world. A false icon? It is a truth for both science and religion.

Many of your people have died for and because of a particular view of life. Yes. They have become a people of priests to the nations, and the tabernacle is the human heart. A false hope? What better grip will we ever have on reality save through our own human experience? A false hope? It is embedded in the depths of human experience. It is the evolution of human experience, part of which we also fashion. For in truth, we are the creators of the reality of our own visions. It is a hope for Arabs and Israelis. It is a hope for Africans and Americans. Habakkuk's vision was real because he believed it would speak and not lie. It was real, for it still empowers a hope that will not die.

*Woe unto him that saith to the wood, Awake; to the dumb
stone, Arise, it shall teach! Behold, it is laid over with gold
and silver, and there is no breath at all in the midst of it.
But the Lord is in his holy temple: let all the earth keep
silence before him.*

In truth, in very truth I tell you. It is a hope for believers and unbelievers. It is a hope for all people of the world. I pray for its success.

Respectfully yours,
Duane Broxson

March 27, 1995
Central High School
6180 Central School Rd.
Milton, Fl. 32570-8545

AMERICAN MUSEUM OF NATURAL HISTORY
Central Park West at 79th Street,
New York, N. Y. 10024,
Attention office of the Editors.

Dear Editors

Re: The Unnatural Moment, "Shoeflies"

The photograph was especially moving to me, but I was stunned by
the caption on this page of Natural History Magazine; "The Unnatural Moment". Was it an unnatural moment of natural history, or unnatural history of a natural moment? What I saw was a truly profound
picture of nature itself!

Respectfully yours,
Duane Broxson

March 27, 1995
Central High School
Milton, Fl.
32570-8545

DR. STEPHEN JAY GOULD,
Museum of Comparative Zoology,
Harvard University
Cambridge Mass. 02138

Re: The Unnatural Moment, "Shoeflies"
Natural History Magazine
March, 1995

Dear Dr. Gould:

The photograph was especially moving to me, but I was stunned by the caption on this page of Natural History Magazine; "The Unnatural Moment". Was it an unnatural moment of natural history, or unnatural history of a natural moment? What I saw was a truly profound picture of nature itself!

As Lame Deer says in Natural History: "Our Circle is timeless, flowing: it is new life emerging from death-life winning out over death". Or as Omar Khayyam has said in his collection of rhymes.:

> *They say the Lion and the Lizard keep*
> *The courts where Jamshyd gloried and drank deep:*
> *and Bahr'am, that great Hunter-the Wild Ass*
> Stamps o're his Head, but cannot break his sleep.

I sometimes think that never blows so red

DUANE BROXSON. THE TEACHER

The Rose as where some buried Cesar bled;
That every Hyacinth the Garden Wears
Dropt in her lap from some once lovely head.

To some evolutionary biologists our will and the consequences of our culture are unnatural. Sometimes the irony of a moment can help us see from a different perspective our place in the world of nature. We are participators in this thing we call nature and our participation does not remove ourselves from it, or from its consequences.

Duane Broxson
Teacher of Science

This photograph and caption appeared in Natural History Magazine under the title, "The Unnatural Moment". The only title to photos I had *noticed* previously was, "The Natural Moment". It was obviously countering, purposefully or not, what I had been saying about man's activity and nature. The photograph was of butterflies on an old discarded shoe. The butterflies were obtaining salt from the sweat that had been left on the shoe. How an evolutionary biologist could see this as unnatural was hard for me to comprehend. Man created the shoe out of necessity purposefully. Since it was created purposefully by man, it was not part of natural nature. How can that be if we evolved along with every other living thing on earth from the beginning? Back off to the moon somewhere and look back at all of the life on the earth. Where and when did anything a man did become removed from the life processes that are unfolding? The preachers harp on this very thing. Man's activity is not part of what is really natural. He is destroying the perfectly created world because his selfish will is contrary to "nature". I am saying that his selfish will is very much a part of nature and that nature itself could care less what man does. Of course we care and we should, we are conscious, but we are just part of this grand unfolding, but a real part nevertheless. You hear it all of the time. Man is destroying the balances of nature. Well maybe he is. So what. Destroying balances is a natural thing and he is as he destroys. It has happened before. Deer starve when they over populate and over graze. I know it is hard to think of the Empire State Building as part of natural nature but what else could it be? The creation of supernatural man? I guess you could say it's an eyesore on God's perfect creation if you still see things that way.

April 7, 1995
Central High School
6180 Central School Road
Milton, Fl. 32570

DR. STEPHEN JAY GOULD,
Museum of Comparative Zoology,
Harvard University
Cambridge Mass. 02138

Dear Dr. Gould:

Here are some reflections. I hope you will read them.

The Instantaniety of Itself

The conscious mind is a continuous interaction that had its origin at the onset of the life process. That process began in the absence of consciousness in the earliest forms and has progressed through complexity to the higher order interactions which allow consciousness. It came on line gradually and in its various aspects in an already established continuing process. This process goes back as far as our observational abilities allow us to determine, but it actually occurs only now. It is, in other words, continuous we would say. All other processes underlying its existence have also been continuous with it or it would have surely suffered disruption.

What other view can we take of reality other than that projected through our own being as it reflects aspects of itself? We exist as part of the very physical system we try to explain. We are the up quarks, down quarks and truth quarks unfolding continuously but existing only now. Since all aspects of ourselves seem to be proceeding continuously all events exist in simultaniety with themselves. Even though they exist in simultaniety, observations cannot be simultaneous with the observed because they have become symbolic representations of the observed in an ongoing system through informational input from the senses. For sight, we receive photons coming from an object and perceive what photons from the object triggers in the ongoing memory of ourselves.

The mind (in its physical essence) is composed of the very things it tries to describe in conceptual terms. When the interval we are trying to perceive in scientific applications approaches actual instantaniety the ability to form an observation breaks down. It is not just observation interfering with the observed but observation becoming one with the potentially observed. It is here that the mathematical system based upon intervals is unable to describe the reality of interactions, since the conceptual process that establishes the relationship between it and reality is being denied by the necessity of an ever smaller observation interval. When not observing externally the observational system remains simultaneous with what it would observe, and records no symbolic memory of external experiences. When observation becomes simultaneous with what it is trying to observe, it exists as the instantaniety of itself, and forfeits its observational ability. Consciousness then is a process existing simultaneously with the phenomenon it is observing, but recognizing that phenomenon in symbolic form as interactions within the brain after the process of observation. We always see what has happened. We use the symbolic past to create the interval of our consciousness and we project that consciousness beyond the now in existence by that same symbolic interval.

Our system of integers cold be described as a system of intervals for this is how they have been discerned by the conscious system. In viewing any object, it must be recognized by our observational system and held their in the memory system. In order to reach the concept of plurality the existence of individuality must have been recognized in memory. Numerating is just a representation of the process of observational memory proceeding through a series of intervals. The reality of numbers in the conscious mind is really the process that recognizes intervals and did not have its origin in the identification of specific objects, distances and etc. There is an unseen interval between objects as the mind forms the concept just as an interval exists between numbers and represents the mechanism of an observational process. Consciousness did not bring into being the observational process, rather the innate observational process brought consciousness into being. These intervals also become our concept of time as we bring our processes to consciousness by the recognition of a symbolic interval held in memory. Time as we view it is merely a conscious conception that enables our consciousness through the observational interval. In other words, we have created time with the observational interval.

Here lies most of the difficulty with concepts such as the infinite. Symbolic intervals stand in the place of the reality that it has observed and projects itself beyond observational reality by the same process. The question of infinity is a difficulty of the entire system that consciousness uses to construct the reality of itself and not one of specific application. Infinity exists in the conceptual process, it does not *necessarily* exist in the reality of the internally or externally observed phenomenon. The unobserving physical world has no interval. It occurs in the instantaniety of itself. It is simultaneous in all events that shape the whole. Perception requires the establishment of the interval to bring itself to a recognition state that becomes our consciousness. We can perceive our idea of momentum, for example, only through the remembered interval. If the interval becomes instantaneous with itself, we can conceive no momentum for objects. We realize, however, the momentum of objects through the perceived interval of experience. This does not mean no momentum exists. It means that no conscious concept of what we call momentum is possible without an interval, so we create one with our memories. We assign our intervals. Our observations become relative to their origin, reference, and communicating medium.

Relativity allows us to reduce some of the discrepancies that observational systems experience though interpretation of informational signals, but does not refute actual simultaneity. It refutes observational simultaneity ,a big difference.

Consciousness is the bridge that interfaces our internal and external experience. We perceive our own selves through our own time frames of the extended world, as we "see" ourselves with the recognition of observations played upon the workings of our timeless inner-selves. When we turn the senses (both external and internal) off, such as in sleep, we lose our observational input into the perception making process and cease to be conscious. Everything about us continues to function in the instantaniety of itself. When we dream we activate the higher level sorting assemblies of perception that processes actual observational information, without any actual external input, and experience a subliminal type of consciousness, one also being processed through the memory of its experiences. When our life processes cease our observational powers are lost and we become what we always were, timeless existence that brought ourselves to conscsiouusness.

To Jerry Hunter, The Preacher

Out of the searing, surging storms of a nuclear inferno,
Flung across an eternity of galactic time,
Coalescing from the spent remains of a burned out star,
I am.

Red Giant, White Dwarf, Supernova,
All a part of the Great Jehova?
Twinkle, twinkle awesome star,
I am a part of what you are!

I Am

I've seen the snow capped mountains high
And heard the rumbling river's roar,
I've felt the heat of burning fire
And touched the placid waters cool.

I am my failing eyes and ageing face,
I am my joy and tender caring,
I am my fumbling hands and stumbling feet,
I am my hope and future vision.

I am the battered driftwood of a thousand storm wrecked ships,
I am the memory of a thousand battles won.
I am the rageing fire of every tyrant's sword,
I am the pleasant peace of all men's spirits gentle.

Letters

I am the subtle star light of every one I've known,
I am my self the burning noon-day sun,
Here and now is what I am,
Now and when is what I will be.

I am a moment of a place in space and time,
I rest among a billion unnamed stars.

Respectfully yours,
Duane Broxson

July 28, 1995
Central High School
Milton, Fl.

FOLKLORIST ROGER L. WELCH
Welch Tree Farm
Dannebrog, Nebraska

Dear Mr. Welch:

Pardon me for my light science. "Humans are not the end result of predictable evolutionary progress, but rather a fortuitous cosmic afterthought, a tiny little twig on the enormously arborescent bush of life", as Dr. Gould would say.

I would repeat this about a thousand times, but I don't have a computer here to help me with my disciplinary assignment. Strange as it may seem though, in my logical mind, I have not really viewed it in any other way. My view is that man is nature. All of him, not just his DNA. Microtubules and all are included. To think that animal culture is unnatural appears to me to also be a misconception. Joshua struck out the idea of an unnatural human culture somehow working above and beyond true nature which seems, to some, to end at conception. It had nothing to do with any pseudo science movement.

"Behavior in highly social, intelligent animals is not only genetically coded but also learned from elders and peers and thus culturally transmitted."

Various measures are being tried, such as trenches along the boundary where forests meet cultivated fields and installing electrified fences, all with only limited success so far. Any solution that seeks to accommodate both elephants and people will have to be based on respect for the intelligence of these highly social creatures, which are capable of creative responses to new solutions.

Letters

*Nature, and we as a part of nature are at risk. The explosion
in the New Mexico desert is said to have created its own
meteorological micro environment Lightning and gales
heralded the arrival of the new age. Let us hope our
inheritance will be one of light and not of wind..*

Scientists hope. Faith that righteousness will prevail is a hope, not a hypothesis, not a theory about what will happen when all of the fortuitous events that will concern mankind have taken place, or that any specific event will happen. A hope is a sunrise, a dawning, that gives a purpose for the day, where none seemed to exist before. A hope is a creator not an explainer. It creates new avenues for human behavior.

I have no connection to any movement of intelligent design for nature. I know nothing of their organization and have no desire or intent to make an iceboat, or spin doctor anything (maybe fortuitously!) for anyone to ride in. Man, in his small world, dabbles in intelligent design in his interactive sphere. If some of it should be able to benefit all life (like keep them from becoming history, if that could be called good for them) why not try? Why not have this for a hope and a purpose? We are purpose makers you know. I know this much, if I know nothing else. I would rather live in a world of tolerance among humans and for other species, than be threatened by the selfish "evil", but natural design, of an Adolph Hitler. Oops! Unless by my inheritance, I too, happened to find myself on that particular band wagon. I don't think the men who invaded Normandy felt very warm and fuzzy, but violence in either direction doesn't seem to intelligently solve many of the problems that might just be solvable if we tried hard enough.

Shucks! I should have just written the damn thing a thousand times. In your view, I'm right back where I started from, Unnatural man tampering with natural nature! "Yeah, sure, right, uh-huh."

Duane Broxson

October 20, 1995
Central High School
Milton, Florida 32570

SCIENTIFIC AMERICAN, INC.,
415 Madison Avenue,
New Your, NY 10017

Dear Editors

Re: God's Utility Function:

"Humans have always wondered about the meaning of life. According to the author, life has no higher purpose than to perpetuate the survival of DNA".

"Genes don't care about suffering, because they don't care about anything."

"DNA neither cares nor knows. DNA just is. And we dance to its music."

It is a two way street. DNA and experience coexist. The function of DNA cannot be isolated from its experience. In the first life, was it the molecules interacting for their survival, or was the conditions of their continued experience just a part of a greater experience? Energy flows one way in the life process. The first molecules did not have affinities for their survival. They just had affinities and their experiences fashioned their continued existence. Experience was just as much a player as the DNA itself.

DNA has a part in its own experience. The feedback cycle has always been present. It has further and more complexly manifested itself in the human will. Man is surely nature, as sure as any other life form is nature. Feedback that has produced will has produced a purpose maker. The purpose maker, being nature, can also change to some extent the course of nature by his own choosing. Man can interact

Letters

with DNA with will in the twenty first century!

DNA dances to the music of its experiences just as we dance to the music of our own DNA. Obviously, man's sphere is a small part of the enormity of life. Nevertheless, man with will does interact with DNA and becomes part of its "experiences". *E. Coli* can make insulin now.

The feedback cycle continues. Man has the power with will to modify some of lifes' experiences, influencing forever the course of some of life's natural history, even his own! In man's own experiences with will, he has come to the collective realization that some of his experiences produces unnecessary suffering as he reflects upon it. Within the realm of nature and by the hand of nature itself, the idea of suffering has manifested itself. Man has been able to integrate into his collective conscious experience of his own choosing. Whether we like to believe it or not those experiences have a definite influence on some DNA in the 21st Century. It is enough to change forever the course of some of life's natural history. It is interesting to contemplate how much of the course of natural history will be determined by the purposeful action of a natural man.

Human purpose is now where it has always been, in the imaginations, ruminations and actions of the human spirit, which has unfolded and interacted as all of nature has unfolded and interacted, being an integrated part with oneness in the reality of all of nature. Nature herself has called up a purpose maker. The purpose maker himself will be subject to all of his own experiences as they play themselves upon the unfolding score of all nature's music.

Respectfully yours,
Teacher of Science

February 28, 1996
Central High School
Milton, Fl. 32570

AMERICAN MUSEUM OF NATURAL HISTORY
Central Park West at 79th St.,
Office of the Editors
New York, NY

Re: This View of Life: Microcosmos, Stephen Jay Gould

Dear Editors·

The hand still points toward the stars. Oxygen and sulfur and all of
the heavier elements have their origin in the "life" cycle of great stars.
The radioactive elements that heat the earth were also formed in the
great blasts of "dying" stars. To say that "The energy to power this
ecosystem did not come from the sun, either immediately or ulti-
mately" obscures the real source of energy for the sun and all of the
other processes that have proceeded from it. After all, that bacterial
biomass hidden in the cleft of the rock owes even the possibility of its
existence to the evolution of stars.

Yours respectively,
Duane Broxson
Teacher of Science

February 28, 1996
5882 Cedar Tree Dr.
Milton, Fl. 32570

DR. STEPHEN JAY GOULD,
Museum of Comparative Zoology,
Harvard University
Cambridge Mass. 02138

Dear Dr. Gould:

It was always hard for me to grasp how such concentrations of the heavier elements blown off from ancient, ancient stars could have been present in sufficient quantity to form the earth and planets at the same time the sun began fusing hydrogen from the same star-forming nebula. Heavier elements up to iron are hypothesized to have formed in the cores of evolving stars and heavier radioactive elements in the shock wave of a supernova blast. What are the probabilities of accumulating such a large amount of radioactive material and heavier material in the body of the earth such as to compose and heat the earth six billion years after its formation, and billions and billions and billions of years since these elements were blown off at extremely high speeds into every direction in space? I am aware of the extremely long half life for many of these heavier radioactive elements. This led me to consider, years ago, that possibly the sun was an ancient binary or some similar structure that went through an as yet unexplained blow off and accretion that led to the formation of orbiting bodies near the sun that contained these radioactive materials as well as concentrations of the other heavier elements. Such a possibility also fits well with the present observed features of our solar system such as the compositions of the inner and outer planets, orbits of comets and etc. Are the heavier elements in the star forming nebulas, as recognized by their spectra, great enough to account for these concentra-

DUANE BROXSON. THE TEACHER

tions? If a planet coalescing from the nebula concentrated heavier elements, wouldn't the sun also coalesce these elements when it began its formation from the same nebula? What happens to this material? I know that matter exists as plasma in the cores of active stars. Is it possible that some of the materials of the inner solar planets actually represents portions of the original cores of some ancient stars or of some material from the core of an ancient binary or of some ancient star- like structure yet unknown?

Yours truly,
Duane Broxson

April 4, 1996
5882 Cedar Tree Dr.
Milton, Fl. 32570

FOLKLORIST ROGER L. WELCH,
Welch Tree Farm
Dannebrog, Nebraska

Re: "Monkey Business"

Dear Sir:

You are expressly correct. We will not settle these issues of science and theology by debate or by expressing our dogmatic views about bible, prayer or God. Yes, your Indian friend is correct in my view. It should be a life in which every moment is a wonder and a prayer of gratitude to all that sustains us in this life.

Power and control have corrupted both the visions of Isaiah and Jesus. Today in some Christianity, we have rich social clubs and Christian Pharisees spouting their religious dogma, which usually boils down to, "see it like I see it", placing the emphasis upon imposing a doctrinal belief system instead of Jesus's emphasis of living it within a life system.

The whole of the bible is a unique glimpse of the evolution of human experience and perspective which continues to this day. There we can view in retrospect some of the grand players and contemplate their intent and influence. Is it a coincidence that the tabernacle of the God of the Jews was moved from a tent, to a building, to the heart of a man, or was this a reflection of the evolution of human experience and culture and the influence that its key players had on that culture and experience? All that we humans can seem to call "good" for us

DUANE BROXSON. THE TEACHER

can be seen unfolding in such experiences as these. Is it a coincidence that the God of the Jews moves from a God of vengeance and wrath to one of tolerance and love, or was this a reflection of the evolution of human experience and culture, and the influence that its key players had on that culture and experience?

Our views and visions are widening. We are gradually casting off our "territoriality of the mind-set". We are beginning to view the oneness of all life again, afresh, from a new perspective. Not viewed as one of domination and special creation, but one of oneness in the path of life, in the scheme of things. One that is of shared joy and despair. I really think tears of joy would flood down the face of Jesus if he looked out and saw Christians, and those of the faith of Islam, and Israelis of all of all kinds of faith, and those of all other faiths, embracing each other in a spirit respect, concern, tolerance and love for one another, their dogmatic differences of history and preference evaporated by the genuineness of their acceptance, concern and caring for one another. The Holy Tabernacles attached to their specific cultural aspects and physical territories melted in the caring respectful concern of the tabernacle of the heart, as Isaiah and Jesus envisioned it. Surely Jesus shared Isaiah's vision for he was a literal enactment of parts of it by his own choice. Isaiah's vision expanded to include all humanity and has been carried there by Jesus the Master Servant. Jesus was aware of this. He read the scrolls of Isaiah. He knew full well what mission he had chosen to take upon himself, whether one views him as a God or a mere man. He read the lamentations and cries of Isaiah for the people of his heart and embraced his vision and his hope. He became a part of an evolutionary human experience influencing not only the social and cultural aspects of humanity but all of life due to the consequences of those social and cultural changes.

Have we not cried out at the terrible tragedy in the Balkans as we cried out at the holocaust? Is it not those experiences that have the most influence on melding the hearts of humanity? Violence in either direction nurtures selfish vengeance. We can see this in the Middle East. Can love grow where the blood fell?

One thing we must remember. Science is an activity of the whole man. The whole man gives purpose and intent to his science. I pray for the spirit of Jesus and its influence on the whole man. The name of Jesus will take care of itself.

Respectfully yours,
Duane Broxson

TIME MAGAZINE LETTERS
Time and Life Building
Rockefeller Center,
New Your, N.Y. 10020

Re: "Why We Need to Raise Hell"

Jack E. White says in his article "Why We Need to Raise Hell": "The main obstacle to integration is not race but class."...... "If it takes new turmoil to bring that about, that is a price we should be willing to pay."

The problem, however, seems to be one of both race and class. Race amplifies the problem. It adds another dimension to an already established process. Discrimination, unfortunately, is part of our social and cultural inheritance within the white race alone, and it will probably remain in some form for ages to come. Upward mobility and educational attainment among whites themselves, depends more upon social skills and socioeconomic status than any other factor, including intelligence. This is true because those attributes greatly increase a person's ability to expedite his own individual interests through the social contacts they bring about. Discrimination occurs continuously in this context within the white race alone. Who should expect it to be eliminated across a racial barrier? It is only amplified.

No such thing as a classless society exists. In American culture the boundaries are just broader and more indistinct. The key and unifying principle which can sustain our society amid all of the turmoil of race and class is the unquestionable worth of all individuals across

Letters   245

all races and across all classes. This was the vision of our founding fathers. This was the vision of Abraham Lincoln. When this becomes truly part of the heartbeat of America, class will not loom so large, race will not loom so large and the disruptive effects will diminish. Each aspect will find itself recognized as a meaningful part of the whole. This vision is not passed on by raising hell in the streets, but by rearing good children in good homes. It takes place in the homes, churches and workplaces in the communities and cities of our Nation. It is passed on from generation to generation in the value systems that are taught to the children of its land. We have enough black and white Christians in our land to make a real difference in this respect, if they would just take their Christianity seriously. What we don't need is more black hatred heaped upon the white hatred that does exist among some of our people.

Abraham Lincoln was a man of great vision and compassion for humanity. He was also a realist. He once asked the question: "How many legs will a sheep have if you call his tail a leg?" The answer given was five. "You are mistaken," said the President, "for calling a tail a leg does not make it one."[1] He was relating this to give insight into his problem of emancipation. We cannot eliminate the strife between classes or races by mere laws or decrees. We can, however, emancipate all classes and all races from their destructive grip on each other by showing genuine worth and caring for all Americans regardless of class, race or station in life. I believe Lincoln, more than any man, wrestled with the stark realities of the difficulties that lay ahead for the emancipated black man in America. If he were here now, would he be trying to make them white? Would he be trying to eliminate class? Rather, I believe, he would realize these as far fetched improbabilities. He would, however, recognize a poor black man and a poor white man as his equal in worth because he had risen in his own mind above prejudice toward race and prejudice toward class though he recognized the inevitability of race and class. This is what we really need as our founding fathers envisioned it. When the doors of the heart open, the doors of the schools automatically open. Some of us could have opened them years ago without any court injunctions. All Americans should recognize their differences for what they are and strive hard to become brothers in this nation of great diversity. When this becomes a reality in the collective conscious of the masses of Americans, America will become one, regardless of race, religion, class, gender or station in life.

We will integrate some but not all. We will remove the burden of class for some, but not for all. We can, however, strive to be a brother to all. He should be my black brother whether he lives with me or apart from me. I should be his white brother whether I live with him or apart from him. We should be brothers whether we go to his school, my school, or our school. I should be his brother whether I am rich or poor, white or black. He should be my brother whether he is rich or poor, white or black. This is the real American dream. Then we should all be "free at last."

Yours truly,
Duane Broxson

May 28, 1996
5882 Cedar Tree Dr.
Milton, Fl. 32570

DR. DAVID SLOAN WILSON
State University of New York,
Binghamton, N. Y.

Dear Dr. Wilson:

I read in Natural History's "Evolution's New Heretics", May 1996 about your interest in group selection. I am not familiar with all of the formal writings and hypotheses on these various issues. I have given some thought to the principle of Darwinian selection and share some of your ideas about group selection. I have not approached these considerations from an empirical standpoint as would be required of an objective scientist but more from an intuitive or theoretical approach. I would like to share with you some of my thinking on this matter. I realize a layman has little to offer specialized scientists in their field but thought you might like to read the stories anyway.

> *It's not surprising that Wilson and Sober want to see human altruism as the result of group selection," He says, "Many people do. The discovery that some altruism isn't genuinely altruistic but is instead fundamentally selfish is deeply disturbing. Some would find comfort if we were able to reconcile our moral feelings with biological reality, but unfortunately it seems we can't." Nesse argues that we have to accept this reality and not seek to change the science to suit our feelings.*

One of the great insights that is going to come out of group selection is that morality will be justified at face value.

Did Darwin overlook or omit man's conscious will in formulating his ideas of Natural Selection? Does conscious will add a new dimension to the underlying thinking that has formulated Darwinian evolution?

When did conscious will stop being a natural player in the interaction of all life? When Darwin, in passing, referred to some aspects of it as "Artificial Selection"? Was it when our view of the evolution of all life became limited to individuals in the species sense? Surely our moral feelings are part of biological reality. How can they be separated from it? The clearer biological reality is that man's conscious will is natural and with will the "progression" of nature can be changed. We being nature have become conscious "lawmakers" in deed and word. One reiterating the other. Our conscious will is as much a part of the evolution of nature as any other aspect is a part of that evolution.

Our consciousness is part of a process that selects behaviors that we want to be expressed and suppresses behaviors that seem to be detrimental and offensive to us. We fashion the mood of the over-all collective conscious with the acquired "genes" of learned experiences which interacts with aspects of personality and the emotion. Just as the unconscious aspects of the physical world "selects" through selection mechanisms, our consciousness "selects" those behavior that are to its perceived collective best interest. Consciousness becomes subject to its own "laws" of conscious nature. Those "behaviors", as well as our body of knowledge, transmitted by learning and social contact are part of biological reality and the consequences and experiences they bring into play affects all life on every level. Just think, *E. Coli* can make insulin now.

Biological evolution does not stop with the interaction of genes on the molecular lever. Selection pressure mechanisms alone have shown us this. Genetic information finds its way into the gnome and then by all aspects of sexuality is transmitted to the offspring of the species. Now in the twentieth century for many species, including our own, the innate and unlearned as well as much of the learned behavioral aspects of sexuality can be bypassed through conscious will. This is an exciting if not frightening thought. One that would tend to cause us to think "unnatural". Many have called it "artificial" selection. But guess what? Nature is evolving, and by our own hand in some regards. This we can be sure of in terms of genetic engineering. The truth of this is marching on very quickly!

In the standard model, organisms produce more offspring than can survive. Organisms possess natural variations. (The basis for all evolution) Competition takes place between them where by only the "fittest" pass on their genes to future generations as determined by their experiences. There is a struggle for survival on the part of the individual. (I feel it is not a struggle for survival but just a picking for its historically evolved craving. Survival being a fortuitous afterthought.) Therefore, the author of the diversity of all life is just selfish competition. Selfish competition however, is not the only experience that an organism will face as it picks for its historically evolved craving. What happened to chance? What about pure damn luck? What about cooperation? What about man's will and his ability to use it to change nature? What about man's will and its cooperative aspects? What are the possible sources of variation in the first place? All of experience is as much a part of evolution as the DNA itself. We create experiences, with will, that defines fitness for some aspects of nature. Darwinian evolution by natural selection in terms of just "red in tooth and claw" is a very simplistic view of life as grand and diverse in ways and means as we are able to observe it in this view of life.

The profound and concerned (rightfully so) naturalists cry out: "Man is destroying all nature's balance and threatening the integrity of his own relationships within the ecosphere!" Man is destroying nature by his own unnatural hand! Man is disrupting the balances of nature as if nature had a predetermined course it was going to take before man disrupted it. Man is polluting nature with all of his synthetic and unnatural creations and activity that are not a part of true nature as they see it! What, however, is one balance or the other, or any balance at all for that matter to nature, other than in the ruminations of consciousness?

When did the activities of man become unnatural? When he began making choices with will which can defy simple Darwinian principle? Was it when he began to integrate his consciousness with the consciousness of others forming dynamic and interacting networks of feedback response? When did he become supernatural? Was it when he colored the perspective of his own interactive experience with "good" and "evil".

Twentieth century science has disclosed man's physical oneness with all of nature down to the very molecules of all life. His conscious will, however, to some, becomes unnatural even though his consciousness arrived through the activities of the very nature he seeks to explain. A bird can sit on a fence and plant trees and that and everything the bird does is natural, but the fence is unnatural?

Why all of this discussion about what is natural? I feel many evolutionary biologist refuse to recognize the fact that all animal behavior is natural from the simplest affinities of the molecules, to the grand activities of man's intuitive will. They admit we all evolved from the same primordial chemical soup can of all life through the same processes and with the same materials and energy as all other life, but they are still stuck on, as Darwin would put it, artificial selection, denying the true nature of man's conscious will.

Why is the naturalness of human consciousness and activity important? It is important because it allows us to see that every aspect of life, including all of the activities and characteristics of man, have unfolded within and are an integral part of the whole biological system. There is no supernatural aspect to man's consciousness. It exists as part of and within the biological system of planet earth which is in turn part of the evolution of the universe itself. We are creation and consciousness. And consider this, human consciousness and will is not by itself among the diversity of life on this earth! Choice is not new. It has evolved from simple innate choices to the complex choices of man within the life system itself. As a matter of fact, without all those millions of years of interacting and unfolding, human consciousness and will would not be possible!

Nature itself, has produced through natural processes a purpose maker! Everything man does is natural! Even his subjective manipulation of nature itself! It is exciting to contemplate that true nature has not limited the complexity and beauty of life to a simplistic Darwinian survival of the fittest, red in tooth and claw, aspect because the conscious will of man is a real and natural player in the natural unfolding of things. In his own realm he has become a purpose maker! He can with will change forever the course, and does, that some aspects of nature will take! His cries of deepest agony are natural. His exhilaration and joy are natural! Human behavior from sex to politics to religion is natural and have their influence on the course nature will take on planet Earth in the twentieth century. Just because we cannot see clearly how some aspects of human behavior fit into the scheme of Darwinian evolution of individual fitness does not exclude its influence. It suggests an even more complex unfolding of things that we need to investigate.

Some merely reflect that man is a small blip on the enormous tree of life in an equally enormous universe. A dead end that will pass away while the life process continues on. It is quite possibly true. That remains to be seen (by someone other than ourselves hopefully). Well, we couldn't really see it ourselves anyway. Surely it has been the case for most of life as we define species. The unfolding of natural history to this point, however, has included man and it can never be what it would have been without him. Might our dead end just be our present

view of species? Haven't we in some ways corrupted our own definition of species? I also understand some dinosaurs might have evolved
into birds of the twentieth century!

I believe human morality has a biological basis because everything
a man does has a biological basis. Even his thoughts have a biological basis. Human morality is biological, not in the sense that we can
deterministically find a gene for some aspect of human morality, but
within the congruence and oneness of all life and its interrelation-
ships with all aspects of that process.

Just think. Imagination and the outcomes it can produce are natural!
Could imagination in creative ways destroy forever some of the "laws"
of nature that we have deduced from the limited view we have of all
nature? An "Adolph Hitler" could gain control of the human element
and with his knowledge and ability change forever the course of some
of natural history. He did. This too has been called unnatural by some.
A "Jesus Christ" could come and touch the hearts of millions of individuals and change the course of some of natural history. He did. How
exciting and fascinating are the prospects for mankind, formulator, to
some extent, of his own destiny and the destiny for many others within
the life system. Truly we have become purpose makers in our small aspect of life on this earth. We have become empathizers and that natural
empathy has a part in the scheme of things. Our purposes have become
part of the purposes for nature, for we are that nature.

Over the eons of the recollected and reconstructed history of our consciousness that we call time, we have viewed the victories and defeats,
the heartaches and despairs, forming and fashioning the temperament
of our own collective consciousness. Amid some of our grandest visions for the hope of mankind, we have cried out in exasperation and
hopeful expectation: "What sends us?" Surely we can here the answer
reverberating down through the pages of our recollected history: "I
am that I am has sent us", for we are in the reality of things both cre-

ation and consciousness.

Yours truly,
Duane Broxson
Teacher of Science
cc Stephen Jay Gould

DR. STEPHEN JAY GOULD,
Museum of Comparative Zoology,
Harvard University
Cambridge, Mass. 02138

Dear Dr. Gould:

I recently read "Creating the Creators". What a clear, beautifully written, scientific requiem for a sequentially progressive view of evolutionary biology by simple Darwinian selection alone. But do we see it all?

My inner soul intuits a glimmer from deep within my inner emotional self that seems to rekindle the fading flickers of a beloved tradition. A tradition to be revisited for sure, but one that has origins as old as the process of life itself, for my heart beats with the energy of that first life and I am an expression of that life force unfolding in the complexity of its' now, humbled by its' perceived insignificance, but emboldened by its ability to form visions, to practice creativity and fashion and form the very unfolding of part of nature.

Should one write a requiem for the hope of righteousness for mankind and all life? I know from your own writings that you are not trying to do so. And I could not if I wanted to. My goal is not to manipulate known ideas into a formulation that allows a fit with some preconceived prejudice, but to search for that factor of the essence, for that part of its life-pulse that has allowed my soul, my consciousness, and yours, to fill with a hope, a joy, not seen in "red in tooth and claw".

The quantum state is an enigma. A state where observation teases out an outcome from a poorly understood preexisting potential. Are we doing just that with some aspects of our own manipulation of nature? Can we, with our observations and enactments, tease out of our universe a preexisting but obscure reality which we can innately feel, certainly experience, but not understand or explain? Being the most knowledgeable scientist that you are (sincerely), you know and understand the limitations of science. We know our knowledge is incomplete, and must be revisited, restated or changed altogether as new insights unfold. This dynamic aspect has made science great and this is what gives me hope, even in the light of science, for a world and a nature that can somehow rise above the known reality of "red in tooth and claw". The Biblical visions do just that. They prod and tease our conscious selves to not only see nature from a different perspective but to make it different by the willful enactment of real life experiences. We know our personal "God" is what we make it. Even Biblical writings teach that. We know science has discredited much of the religious traditions of all faiths, but has it discredited that essence, that driving force that has sparked men's lives and souls to strive for what we call righteousness? Could it? After all the expressions of righteousness become part of experience. Experience, willful or otherwise, has its affect in the real world of nature.

To some extent, believe it or not, I have been given the ability to see through the eyes of science (by my physical inheritance and my experiential inheritance), but I have also been given the ability to see and feel through the reality of my inner self and its relationship to all other life. It too realizes its dual potential, but through the experiences of others and itself, that hope for righteousness manifests itself. What is its essence? A learned experience? An inherited, preconceived prejudice? An absurd notion? Just the "is" of the real world? A contemplated choice based on experience? Whatever its origin, it is a manifest expression of nature, for we are that essence; that supernova generated carbon atom, that sequence of nucleotide, that arrangement of amino acids, that interaction of proteins, that discerner and manipulator of the physical world, that destroyer, that creator, that empathizer, that life-pulse, that quantum leap.

I must admit, in view of industrialization, the human population explosion, exploitation of the environment and religious and political bigotry, the view seems dim for us and much of the other life on planet Earth. It seems much like the development of a supernovae explosion, or the maturing of one of those great Gulf Coast thunderstorms. It builds to its maximal level of complexity and then crashes as the energy source that sustains it is depleted. Complexity also narrows the range of future experience that will be favorable to sustain it. Since complexity integrates many, many interactions, the welfare of the whole becomes dependent upon many specific conditions, just one of which if significantly disturbed might mean the demise of the whole. We can see evidence of this in our records of the life that came before, for extinctions of branches seem to be the rule rather than the exception. For blind innate activity proceeding toward complexity, the end result appears inevitable, but the added dimension of insight gives us a glimmer of hope.

I have often contemplated the redundancy of higher forms' DNA. I can understand how "null" pieces of DNA or extra copies of functional DNA might find their way into the genome of an organism. I wonder sometimes though about a different possibility for some of this redundant DNA. The instructions encoded within the DNA molecule are directly related to a sequence of events that occur within and outside of the nucleus. Feedback systems are obviously at work between the nucleus, cytoplasm, cell membrane and the external environment, each aspect contributing to the sequence of events that thereby unfold in what we consciously call time. Possibly, reacting to conditions arising in such a sequence of events, an encoding segment might be "turned off" as a favorable response to a changed presenting condition without being deleted. If such scenarios as this took place,

Letters

the DNA would hold instructions for building proteins that were necessary in previous periods and conditions of its evolutionary history but are no longer functional. Some of that redundant DNA might well be a record of previous structures or reaction pathways which taken at the time of their unfolding, represented a part of the organism in its previous form. "Is there locked in the redundancy of our own DNA a video tape of our ancient past ready for us to play back on the video player of our genetic knowledge and computer technology"?

Could it be that some of the nonsense sections of DNA we read about today were not nonsense then? I realize that certain amino acid combinations might not be possible. What amino acid forms might have existed then that we do not realize now? Or what possibilities exist that we have not discovered? What timing mechanisms are at work between what happens in the nucleus and its influence thereafter? Is the redundant DNA also part of a timing mechanism?

Since the unfolding of complex multicellular life is a dynamic process that occurs embryologically in time, repeated in time, the nature of an organism is an interaction of a self directing sequence of events superimposed upon an undirected sequence of other events such as environmental changes. At any one time this sequence of reactions and interactions work in concert to produce the physical and interactive state of the organism.

To have a memory bank of genes to study is just part of the picture and is not enough to recreate an organism as it once was. One would need the cellular constituents of the zygote and its membranous and chemical structures and a compatible environment to go with it. One would need to know how genes work in concert with hundreds of other genes and all of the other structures and interactions that influence those genes. The sequence in time would be necessary to bring about the proper unfolding. Even to start with a zygote is to start well along in the process of life that has unfolded.

I wonder if it has occurred to many investigators that the cellular membrane and many of the cellular parts and materials are just as continuous as the replicating nucleus? Receptor and transmitter proteins located within the membranes are like switches and pathways of memory that influence the activities of the cell. All of the membrane memory, physiological memory pathways and chemical memory mechanisms are not lost in a simple cell division but are continuous and transmitted as are the codes of memory located in the nucleus. They help maintain the stable transition from cell to cell. After the DNA produces an RNA code for producing a protein, many interactions occur that are not specifically controlled by the activity of the nucleus.

At the end of a worksheet on the origin of life and the geologic time table, I asked the question: "Do you think that man was a part of all you just read or did he appear in the beginning just as he is now"? An overwhelming majority responded, "Just like he is now". A few thought that man was apart of all they had read. Some did not know. One girl wrote that God and Jesus had created man in the Garden of Eden just like he is now and for man and science to try to understand creation was like trying to eat soup with a fork. I laughed to myself at the truth in that statement. Trying to understand our world is sometimes like trying to eat soup with a fork. It has taken us a long time but the soup level is dropping.

I would like to think that I have had a small part in helping people understand about their world through the eyes of science. I know these people. They are hard working, good and honest people. They have probably given me more than I have given them. It would be an even graver error for man to destroy their hope for righteousness. Christianity should embrace new enlightenments. Science should not reject them with arrogance. After all, we are both creation and consciousness.

I thank you for the education that you have given me over the years through "This View of Life". Believe it or not, I cherish that understanding that you have enabled me to have of evolutionary biology.

Yours truly,
Duane Broxson

March 3, 1997
5882 Cedar Tree Dr.
Milton, Fl. 32570

DR. STEPHEN JAY GOULD,
Museum of Comparative Zoology,
Harvard University
Cambridge, Mass. 02138

Der Dr. Gould:

It is heartening to note that some of the great thinkers of science are willing to engage in respectful discourse, about science and religion, and for one to admit that he can *believe* in something, apart from the factual aspects of empirical science, with all of his heart.

There would be no conflict between science and the church if, in fact, one could say that science lives and functions in one world and religion lives and functions in another. Non-overlapping Magisteria really implies that science and religion could restrict their teaching and influence to intellectual domains while the common man and his society continue unaffected in both worlds with business as usual. For the most part, this has been the case for Christianity in Western Civilization after the center of scientific inquiry moved from the Mediterranean to Northern Europe after the inquisition of Galileo. Certainly Darwin shook the foundations of Christianity's magisteria and produced a "you see it your way, we'll see it our way " view about the origin of the species. The Industrial Revolution shifted much of the art of the artisan and craftsman to science of the machine and engineer, further removing science from its personal touch with the heart of the masses where religion finds its expression. The mainstream of evolutionary biology as a body of individuals did not become part of the layman's church and forfeited its influence there on the credibility of its science. Certainly enlightened religious leaders began to question many of the hard-held traditions of the faith of the masses, but "lay Christianity" built defensive walls around its magisteria, becoming critical of its own higher institutions of Christian theology. The great thinkers and challenging ideas of science and Christianity became isolated in their university enclaves. Science and the Church allowed this non-overlapping magisteria to proceed, though at the heart of the matter were deep and unresolved conflicts.

For a while it seemed that science would obliterate most of the credibility that any religion might seem to have. Physicists and chemists began to see into some of the basic fabric of our universe (both large and small) and began to think that its total comprehension was now within their grasp. It was held impossible for the influence of phenomena to be here and to be there without passing through the time interval of man's own consciousness. That very science, however, which seemed to humble with its power the great visionaries of religion soon found its own self on its knees. It was humbled when it saw that its analytical methods and procedures had limitations beyond which things seemed unknowable; where strangeness, uncertainty, non-locality, and doubt abounded; when the most successful and reliable scientific analytical theory opened wide doors of metaphysical contemplation, about science; when the time line collapsed on itself and revealed its true nature as the mechanism the mind uses to bring its universe into the realm of its own consciousness.

Caught between the magisteria of science and the magisteria of religion is an overwhelming mass of common ordinary people living within the confines of their social and cultural traditions, that are constantly challenged on all sides by conflicting opinions. The power of science and the Information Age of the late twentieth century have melted the isolation produced by the two great magisterias. Their boundaries are engaging as the masses begin to comprehend and experience in everyday life some of the great insights of science. Genetic engineering, in vitro fertilization, birth control, abortion, cloning, and tissue processing (all potentially powerful tools of science and possible solutions to pressing needs and problems) have generated great debate about morality and ethics and have brought underlying precepts forward into public view. Behavioral scientists using Darwinian principles have challenged the basic precepts of Christian morality and altruism, while reductionists have attempted to reduce some human behavior to the mere action of a gene. "What shall we teach and where shall we teach it?" has reverberated within the walls of our chambers of justice, legislative halls, churches, and school board rooms. Advances in science have moved into everyday life in such rapid, powerful and profound ways as to force the ultimate confrontation of those deep and well isolated traditions and convictions. No longer can they be quietly brushed aside. Grave and hard decisions loom on the horizon that must be made by an enlightened and knowledgeable people who share a common trust.

All the power and "truth" of science will not stop the impending stampede of the masses of humanity over the precipice of cultural and economic collapse without engaging the religious and moral aspects of human behavior within the boundaries of the common man's world. How we manage the power and influence of science and religion, in this respect, will become one of the most important realities of the twenty first century. The holocaust has shown that man and his science–empty, alone and separated from the heartbeat of a moral mass of humanity–can become a horror beyond imagination. The following excerpt from Dr. Jacob Bronowski's, The Ascent of Man, speaks to this need.

> It is not the business of science to inherit the earth, but to inherit the moral imagination; because without that man and beliefs and science will perish together.
> It is not true that we run our lives by any computer scheme of problem solving. The problems of life are insoluble in this

sense. Instead, we shape our conduct by finding principles to guide it. We devise ethical strategies or systems of values to ensure that what is attractive in the short term is weighed in the balance of the ultimate, long-term satisfaction

Science of the twentieth century, as Pope John Paul II has realized, has brought the magisteria of both science and religion face to face and the vapor from the heat of it all is causing a cloud that obscures good and proper choices for man, his society, and all of life. Hopefully we can pursue this prospect of "respectful discourse". Pope John Paul II has taken a brave and courageous step forward toward the realization of that goal.

It is at interfaces that the mainstream of things becomes different, dynamic and changing. It is at interfaces that new forms arise and new visions are launched. Science and religion, within the moral mass of humanity, must need be in the process of interfacing. Christianity must face new enlightenments. Science must not refute the beauty of Christianity and the hope of its people with rejection and arrogance. Let us calculate, reason, and pray, that astounding things will happen that will be good for mankind and all of earth's life.

Yours truly,
Duane Broxson
Teacher of Science

Central High School
6180 Central School Road
Milton, Fl 32570-9804

NATURAL HISTORY,
Office of the Editors
Central Park West at 79th St.,
New York, N.Y. 10024

Re: War of the World views

Dear Sirs:

Much of the complexity of life is accomplished with the development of the eukaryotic cell. The cell is the basic unit of structure and function for all of multicellular life and it is far from simple. The rest pivots around this central theme. Reflecting on this, why is it any easier to say: "The simplest kind of cellular life arises as a predictable result of organic chemistry and the physics of self-organizing systems wherever planets exist with the right constituents and conditions-undoubtedly a common occurrence in our vast universe", than to say they might continue their complex development in some form toward self awareness?

Isn't it interesting that almost every branch of eukaryotic heterotrophs proceed toward some kind and level of self awareness? We do have one good example of an evolutionary pathway toward complexity that does not seem to lead to self awareness, higher level autotrophic green plants. One out of two for consciousness that we know about isn't bad. I feel strongly that heterotrophy and the progression toward self awareness that we can observe is not just coincidental but predictable. It begins with heterotrophy, mobility and the evolution of choice as I have suggested in other writings.

Letters

If we really want to get basic, we might say: "Behold! The age of the cell", with all of its possibilities, uniting all life of earth in thought as well as ancestry, making it our kind rather than his kind or their kind.

We have only one experiment and revealed as part of that experiment is ourselves. At least we know that the nature of man is possible. That, however, is not all we know. We know that the basic physical and chemical relationships we have been able to formulate here on the earth can be applied in principle to the far reaches of our observed universe. Organic molecules of our own definition, are scattered throughout our observed universe. When we look out, we might expect to find cells. Given the vast dimensions of a universe not totally unknown, we might also expect everything that cells have to offer.

Just think, some where out there in that vast expanse of matter and energy of which the very essence of our being is formed, we might just expect to hear form some oddball expression of cells: "!@#$%^ * ()", which being interpreted means, "Behold I am."

Yours truly,
Duane Broxson
Teacher of Science

March 14, 1998
5882 Cedar Tree Dr.
Milton, Fl.
32570-9806

DR. STEPHEN JAY GOULD,
Museum of Comparative Zoology,
Harvard University
Cambridge, Mass. 02138

Dear Dr. Gould:

How is one inconsequential blip's world view going to affect all of nature and its unfolding save in the realm of the conscious world where it was conceived? We both know that man's social world is ruled by opinion not truth. We both know that man's view of truth and falsehood in his conscious world does not have any influence on the workings of the natural world, save in the experiences that our conscious world brings to bear on the natural world. The experiences that man causes to unfold on the planet is influenced more by opinion than any other aspect. That opinion has a real influence on the workings of nature. Man's conscious world surely brings to bear consequences in the natural world right or wrong, true or false. In fact, I believe that all of this is "natural".

Some would say that one could not have two world views. Does that prevent one from searching deeply into both views for insight into how these relationships have come about in the real oneness of the only world we can conceive? Everything I can conceive as "good" for me and man is caught up in the unfolding of human experience in both of those views.

We have become purpose makers, about this there can be no doubt.

My purpose seems to unfold from a life time of experience both in the emotional and intellectual world. I inherited a love for the people of Israel through my childhood and on into my adulthood because of my unique experiences and culture. I would extend my hopes expressed in this writing[22] to all of the races and cultures enmeshed in the unfolding of human life on earth. Remember, not a rigid doctrine with a questionable basis in truth, but a purpose, a beautiful and good gateway to the future.

Surely when the experiences of the human race are "deleted" by the interaction of the oneness of all nature, it will be a page to be reviewed in another place and by another time.

Yours truly
Duane Broxson

---

[22]The writing "To Israel" was included with this letter.

January 15, 1999
5882 Cedar Tree Dr.
Milton, Florida

DR. STEPHEN JAY GOULD,
Museum of Comparative Zoology,
Harvard University
Cambridge, Mass. 02138

Dear Dr. Gould:

My hat's off to the French chemist. Hope all goes well with the Burgess shale.

Yours truly,
Duane Broxson

Enclosed: An afterthought. ("To the Senate")

October 13, 1999
Central High School
Central School Road
Milton, Fl. 32570

DR. NEIL DE GRASSE TYSON,
Department of Astrophysics,
Princeton University
Princeton, New Jersey 08544-1001

Dear Dr. Tyson:

I had meant to use the comments below as a response to Stephen Jay Gould's article in Time Magazine about creationism. However, after reading your article this month in Natural History Magazine, I decided to share it with you.

I have read many of your articles in Natural History Magazine and have enjoyed and benefitted from your insight and knowledge. I have struggled with these two dichotomies (science and religion) for most of my life. My intellectual life has always embraced science and its wonderfully creative participants, such as yourself. My emotional and spiritual life however, has been steeped in the cultural traditions of home and family and all that we hold dear to our heart. I have loved the literary writings of the Bible since I was a small child. They, like science, have profound things to say to us all. We will always have need of those profound principles of righteousness found there, or suffer the painful process of discovering them again. Their pages reveal the evolving collective consciousness and the influence its will has on the development of the human "spirit". They also help give science direction and meaningful purpose. Through the evolution of life we, with our consciousness and will, have become purpose makers in our realm of influence, not only for ourselves, but for all other life.

DUANE BROXSON. THE TEACHER

The knowledge and wisdom of science is evolving from a sea of human opinion through the application of the principle of the refutable hypothesis. The knowledge and wisdom of Christianity is also evolving from within this same body of human opinion by the application of the principles of righteousness to the experiences of the human will.

Righteousness like science cannot discriminate between truths[23]. That is, it cannot hold to one truth and disavow another. Science and Christianity are bruised when either of these two great insights are ignored. For science, ignoring the principles of righteousness can destroy the noble purpose we have chosen for the science that we seek. For Christianity, ignoring the science established through the testable hypothesis can destroy the credibility of the righteousness that it preaches.

The refutable hypothesis was evolved from human experience just as the principles of righteousness were. Both science and religion have their realms of uncertainty, even now. Certainly all of the ancient traditions of both science and religion were not steeped in "truth" as seen by the eyes of the twentieth century.

Scientists hope for a day when they can better understand some complex aspect of our physical and biological nature. They work diligently with the tools of science to realize that hope. Their work becomes purposeful and influences the progression[24] of our culture.

Christians also hope for a day when the old selfish self of our ancient nature can be significantly modified by the continuous application

---

[23] A "truth" in terms of righteousness could be seen as a principle that the majority of the collective consciousness could agree upon in real life experiences as "good" for mankind and all other life.

[24] Evolutionary biology may not be progressive in its overall influence according to Dr. Gould, but for the human experience we have certainly moved toward more complexity, just as our culture has seemingly progressed toward more complexity, and culture is just as natural a phenomenon as stars. Stars proceed to form from the simpler elements the complex structures that allow the earth and its biological systems.

of those principles of righteousness that have been brought to view by the joys and sorrows of human experience. This process has also become purposeful and has had its influence on the progress of our culture. In the unfolding of nature, the future is not a given. Man with his conscious will participates in the unfolding of nature in his realm of influence.

All science is based upon human experience as seen through the power of its consciousness. Human consciousness, at best, is a second hand experience. It reflects upon the workings of nature from which its very self has become an outcome.

In formulating the methods of science, a process evolved which increased the probability of a desirable outcome, that is, to reveal credible insights into the working and essence of nature, eliminating much of the bias produced by ignorance, cultural tradition, and selfish desire. These desirable outcomes came about gradually as the collective consciousness reinforced itself though the power of its application.

Science was not the only search for a desirable outcome. The experiences that unfolded through the expression of the human will, bathed the collective conscious with joys and sorrows, hopes and despairs and also gradually created a collective desire. A process evolved which would increase the probability of a desirable outcome, one that would thwart unwanted individual selfish desire. It was formulated as a body of moral law that would reinforce the desirable experiences and produce a desirable outcome. For the interaction of human experience it became known as the principle of righteousness that condemned much of the selfish will of a man. It created the notion of good and evil and through the power of the collective consciousness, biased this dynamic interaction toward the "good" of human interactive experience. It is at best an external pressure having its powers vested in the collective conscious, reinforcing the "better angels of our nature".

Is this not, however, an underlying premise for all of biological nature? The experiences of this nature create new experiences, which produce new outcomes, which change underlying influences, which gradually changes the nature of biological nature itself. The interactions of nature gradually writes itself into itself, as into our genome, or for the collective spiritual experience, "writes itself into our hearts", if by some unknown principle we could visualize that, and our individual natures move toward the new defining principles of conscious experience. Oh how the great Biblical prophets of old have longed that it would! How they created the vision of hope for the struggling collective consciousness. Even this process itself seems to unfold as insight leads to insight. "If a man is discovered committing adultery, both he and the other man's wife must be killed; in this way evil will be cleansed from Israel." (Deuteronomy 22:22) Biologically speaking, if a gene for adultery existed, Moses would have taken care of it. But the vision has unfolded, through the countless lives of millions of people, to matters of the personal heart, the personal spirit. "But I say to you, that everyone who looks on a woman to lust for her has committed adultery with her already in his heart." {Matthew 5:27) The Bible envisions a place and a time where "no evil can enter". It envisions a human heart, a human will, a human desire, rewritten by the joys and sorrows, heartaches and despairs of its own continuous experience.

Both science and religion write on the pages of human history. Let us hope that our science will enlighten our religion, and our religion can continue to provide meaningful purpose for our science.

Yours truly
Duane Broxson

From: Broxson, Duane
Sent: Thursday, May
24, 2001 10:59 AM
To: editors@sciam.com

Dear Editors:

Equations do describe what matter does within the appropriate experimental realm. What matter does has written the equations. Consciousness itself, in a way, is what matter does. What equations really can't describe is what matter is, unless, eventually, at the extreme ends of our comprehensible world, what it does becomes what it is.

Worthwhile reality for science with mathematics is limited by observation. Observation is limited by the interval (no matter how small), of what we call time. Observation intervals have brought us to consciousness, for to become aware the mind must create the observation interval. What lies beyond that may never be known, but lets keep trying.

Duane L. Broxson
Science Department Chairperson
6180 Central School Rd.
Milton, Fl. 32570-8545

Though much of the beliefs of the sea hunters is founded in fantasy, as are many "beliefs", the value of those beliefs are imminently obvious, and their understanding of their place in nature reveals a lost insight within the great societies of the twenty first century. I hear our chant ring out throughout our world: "We are the men of the twenty first century, We are the wasteful exploiters of our world." Our hunt is not "holy" and we might not return alive.

Duane L. Broxson
Science Department Chairperson
6180 Central School Rd.
Milton, Fl. 32570-8545

From: Broxson, Duane
Sent: Monday, February 04, 2002
9:13 AM
To: ngsforum@nationalgeographic.com
Subject: "Challenges for Humanity,
A Beginning"

How encouraging it was to read from a great and profound Baptist
Christian the words: "representing millions of years of evolution"[25]

Duane L. Broxson
Science Department Chairperson
6180 Central School Rd.
Milton, Fl. 32570-8545

---

[25] Quoting President Jimmy Carter.

From: Broxson, Duane
Sent: Friday, February 08, 2002
      8:36 AM
To: editorial@discover.com
Subject: Einstein and Godel

Please allow me this reflection for Mr. Berlinski.

A Reflection on Time and Consciousness

Observation intervals have brought us to consciousness, for to become aware, the mind must create the observation interval. The
inherent nature of the universe has no actual past or future; it
exists in the instantaniety of itself. We call the physical world to
consciousness through the creation of the observation interval, as
we recall from symbolic memory in the now the "past" and as
we project in symbolic form, in the now, into the "future". Yes
the physical world interacts, if flows and rearranges itself, but
only in the instantaniety of itself, for the dynamics is created by
consciousness of the observation interval that stores in symbolic
memory the fluxions of instantaneous "nows". Relativity denies
simultaneity, but this is observtional simultaniety. All reality appears simultaneous and instantaneous apart from the application of
consciousness. An "event" is obviously realized only as a creation
of consciousness. The idea of time as we apply it to the system is a
creation of consciousness, and is an essence of consciousness. Our
consciousness exists within an observational reality, encoded in
symbolic memory both in the mind and in script and electronics,
but our physical essence, which is the system, cannot know itself
directly.

Duane L. Broxson

Science Department Chairperson
6180 Central School Rd.
Milton, Fl. 32570-8545

March or April 2002
5882 Cedar Tree Dr.
Milton, Florida 32570

This last correspondence to Dr. Gould was not sent in letter form. It
was written in response to his last article in "This View of Life" in
natural history magazine. I did not know that this was to be his last
article. I knew he was and had been ill with cancer, but I did not know
he was gravely ill. Below is the article as it was sent to Dr. Gould.
It was sent after the writing of "Baseball's Reliquary" but I have no
record of the exact date. It was sometime in late March or early April
of two thousand and two. I knew that Dr. Gould by now realized that
I had some (if not meager) scientific credentials. He knew I embraced
the principles of evolutionary biology. I really thought he couldn't understand how I could embrace two distinct world views. He had seen
some of the science. I wanted him to see how and why I had embraced
the spiritual teachings of Jesus so I sent him this writing. It was written because of him and to him, but it was written from my heart and
my deep spiritual feelings. I wanted him to see a little of my spiritual
heart. I really cannot say what specifically motivated me to include my
writing "Awaiting the African Night". We all face this truth in life. All
of life faces this truth. Even Jesus the Christ faced this truth. The piece
eludes to him if you can see it. One day we will all stand helpless. It
was as if I had unknowingly written a requiem. I love the way the Bible expresses it. "Now the days of David drew nigh that he should die;
and he charged Soloman his son, saying, *I go the way of all the earth*:
be thou strong therefore, and shew thyself a man;". Dr. Gould has gone
by way of all the earth. I will go by way of all the earth. Jesus went by
way of all the earth. And the rest of the story? One thing I know for
sure, his *spirit* still lives within my heart.

He Gave Me His Glove, Mama

Mother:
Where have you been son?

Son:
I've been over at Uncle Grady's house listening to the ball games. We were listening to the Yankees and the Cardinals.

Mother:
The Yankees and the Cardinals?

Son:
Yes mama, Uncle Grady had the Yankees on one radio and the Cardinals on the other old radio that he has.

Mother:
Both games at once?

Son:
Yeah, he does that all the time. He says that this new player Mickey Mantle might one day out shine Joe DiMaggio.

Mother:
Don't count on that son. You know that DiMaggio was one of the greatest players of all time.

Son:
He gave me his glove today mama.

Mother:

You mean that old first-base mitt of his?

Son:
Yes mama.

Mother:
You really love your Auntie and Uncle Grady don't you
son?

Son:
Yes mama, but you know I love you all too, don't you?

Mother:
Sure we do. I sometimes wonder though if Uncle
Grady loves us all as much as he loves those Yankees!
Oh, you know I'm just talking now. Why, he loves
us all as much as we love him. With your Auntie my
sister, and your Uncle Grady your daddy's brother, it's
like you have two mamas and daddies. They can't have
children, you know. And your sister, why, they have
helped us so much with her nurses' school. They love
her so much. Yes, we are lucky, aren't we?

I'm proud he gave you his glove. It was special to him.
Boy! Those Yankees, what great players! You know
son, we have always been Yankee fans. I think it was
because your Uncle Grady worshiped them so much.
They have such great players. It won't be long now
until your daddy comes home from work. We'll have
supper when he gets here. You can tell him then how
the Yankees did today.

Son:
Did you ever hear Uncle Grady tell the story about

Letters

how daddy struck out all those players that time?

Mother:
Why yes son, I've heard that story a hundred times.
Your dad was a good pitcher.

Son:
Do you think dad could have ever played in the Major
Leagues?

Mother:
Who knows son? You know, after the eighth grade he
had to start working. He has worked for his families
ever since. He didn't have a chance to play any ball
like that. Playing wasn't an option for him. But you
know, he never minded because his family was the
most important thing to him. Your dad is such a
special person. He has such a love and respect for
everyone, and yet he is so strong.

Son:
Why doesn't he go to church much mama?

Mother:
Well you know, growing up in the country like he did
and working from day one just to have something to
eat didn't give him much opportunity to come to town
to church or anything like that. Church just wasn't part
of his social life like it was in my family. Your dad
possesses in his heart though, what some people strive
all their life to find.

Son:
Is that why everyone loves dad mom, even Mr Gooden

the colored carpenter that brings the saws by for dad to file?

Mother:
Yes, he is loved and respected by everyone. Your dad has a special heart. He is a special person.

Son:
Do you remember the day the Elders of the church came to visit dad?

Mother:
Yes son, I remember it well.

Son:
Gosh, I was thinking that day, boy, if they really knew my dad, he probably could have helped them understand what they were preaching better.

Mother:
I know son, but they meant well.

Son:
I'll bet Jesus would understand dad, don't you mama?

Mother:
Yes son, I know he would. His is the kind of love that binds us all together. This is the hope of the world son. That the love we have for our families and the respect and goodness that comes from it will someday be shared by all of the people of the world everywhere. You know, that they will be able to get along and have happy lives like we have. This was a hope of Jesus.

Son:

Letters

Mom, wasn't Jesus a Jew?

Mother:
Why yes son, you know that.

Son:
He was a great player too, wasn't he mom?

Mother:
Yes, the greatest, or else we wouldn't have people all over the world today changed by the memory of his teaching from so long ago.

Son:
How is that so mom?

Mother:
Because he tried to teach people to love one another by his vision and example, but not just their families, everyone.

Son:
Did he really rise again mother?

Mother:
They say he did son. But this I know for sure, God is a spirit that lives within us and every time that spirit of the love of Jesus finds its resting-place in the heart of a man to change his vision, Jesus lives again. It's like a nail from that Old Rugged Cross, driven right through our old selfish selves.

Son:
How can that be mama?

Mother:
From soul to struggling soul the flame of the hope of
Jesus is passed and we purge our selfish soul with the
vision of his love. His hope is for our hearts! This is
His Jerusalem!

Son:
You mean the New Jerusalem, mother, that glorious
view of heaven?

Mother:
Yes, the New Jerusalem. He said himself that the
kingdom was within us.

Son:
Wy mama, we've been there all the time haven't we?

Mother:
Yes. Yes son, we've been there all the time. God bless
you son! I love you so much!

Son:
I love you too, mama.

Mother:
Enough of this for now, your daddy will be home soon.
Why don't you go out and play a little baseball with the
boys until he gets back?. And don't get those clothes too
dirty out there in the field.

I can also reverence "A nail from the true cross and dirt from Ebbets
Field". I claim the blessings of both. I have been struggling with the

rational aspects of my Christian Faith most of my life, but it has not diminished my respect for Christianity. He is an icon in his own right, Dr. Gould, but not a fraud. He was no more a fraud that David, Isaiah or Jeremiah was a fraud. Fraud implies an intent to deceive. Can we really decipher out of all of those writings about him a real intent to deceive? Maybe he just understood the nature of the spirit of what we call "God" in the heart of a man better than they did. I don't think Doubleday was involved in any deception. I know you stand "respectfully before such an important item of history and symbol of human cruelty and hope". But it was not cruelty to this man. His agony was also his joy. It was the fulfillment of his vision, the vision of David, Isaiah and Jeremiah. It was a vision for the future, a hope that still unfolds today. The people of Palestine would do well to embrace this "fraud", then maybe they could stop terrorizing and killing each other. But you should know, it is very hard to bend a knee, particularly to what you and many of your people call a fraud. Think of the many people from the past ages and across the globe today, that have been blessed by this man, flesh of your own flesh. Think how the flame of this man has motivated President Carter to do great things for good all over the world. I know you have read those prophecies of a better man, a better nation. I know you have read about putting the spirit of the law into people's hearts. Jesus was the next step. He knew that. He fulfilled it by his own choice.

How hard it is for a rich man, or a proud man, to change his selfish heart (I am not referring to you here, just the teaching). I know something about that and I am certainly not a rich man.

This is about a scene in a National Geographic Video.

Awaiting The African Night

I am a good bird,
Proud and strong,
With my wings,
I soared the shifting currents of rising air,
And glided across the steaming meadows,
searching for a morsel there.

I am a good bird,
Standing tall and sleek,
But a truth comes
Knocking at my door,
His name is Jackal,
And I must fight.

He runs about,
He catches me
From behind,
He snatches
My flight feathers
Off my tail and wing,

I peck and fight,
But my strength is gone,
I stand helpless,
In the dim of evening,
Awaiting the African night.
I was a good bird.

Letters

From: Broxson, Duane
Sent: May 21, 2002 8:29 AM
To: nhmag@amnh.org
Subject: Stephen J. Gould

Please relate my deepest sympathy to Dr. Gould's family and friends.
I share an inexpressible loss.

Duane L. Broxson
Science Department Chairperson
6180 Central School Rd.
Milton, Fl. 32570-85454

Short Stories

The Rattlesnake Head

They came to this place with dogs. They were hunting quail. The dogs were good, they had found many quail. Birds had been flushed, their bolting flutter had lifted them so as to sail silently toward the steep head branch and alight there along its banks in the cover of the gall berry laden swampy thickets. The men walked hurriedly to flush them one by one behind good dogs, almost perfect dogs. The big dog sport winded the small stand of bushes near the head and picked up a brief trail. Suddenly he stopped and stiffened abruptly, head down, tail out stretched, eyes intently locked on the grass before him. He trembled slightly as Duane (his full name meant singing lion) approached from behind with his shotgun ready. As Duane passed the frozen dog, the bird burst into the air with a pounding of its wings and arched up toward the head of the stream. Duane's gun muzzle came up quickly and smoothly and picked up the path of the fleeing quail. Foom! The gun sounded as it crossed the bird on the same path to the somewhere the bird was going. Its wings folded and it began its predetermined arc toward the earth, past the tall bays and juniper, by the titi and gall berry to the moist floor at the head of the steep head stream. Sport was a good dog, but on occasions demonstrated his natural "sinful" desire. Duane loved the dog and knew the dog well. They had hunted many days together. Sport had followed the bird intently with his eyes as the bird arched earthward, but Duane had caught the glimmer in his eyes and the intent in his face. Together they rushed down the steep bank through the brush, crashing through the smilax and bamboo vines to the boggy floor of the branch. Sport was there first. He knew right where the bird had fallen, and his nose did not fail him. He grabbed the bird in his mouth and just as he was about to chomp on the bird, Duane reached him. Throwing down his gun and grabbing him by his mouth and neck, Duane yelled, "G. D. it sport don't you eat that bird." Sport growled as Duane pulled his mouth open and shook the bird out on the ground. "Duane don't!, Uncle Grady called out from the hillside next to the branch, "He will bite you." , but it was too late. Duane already had the bird. Man and dog made up quickly as Duane patted him on his head, thanking him for his work in finding the downed bird, something almost impossible for a man to do in a thick swamp. Sport gagged on a few feathers and looked up at Duane with an expression he had seen so many times, "Ok, you won that one, lets both go and find another one.". Sport started out of the swamp up the steep grade followed much slower by Duane with his bird in his bag and shotgun in his right hand. The bank was steep and hand holds were necessary to climb out. Often the face and neck were barely off the bushy rise of the steep head branch. Out of the swamp, through the thick gall berries, and into an open plowed fire line he crawled. Standing up straight he called out to Grady and Whit, who were standing by watching the episode, a familiar sight to them. "I got it before he could eat it", Duane said. "You sure had better watch out for snakes around here". Grady said. "You could get bit doing stuff like that." Duane had only taken a few steps up the fire line toward Whit and Grady when he saw him there, lying off the fire line in the wire grass and gall berry brush. A big diamond back rattlesnake, One capable of killing you dead on the spot if bitten in the face and neck. "Good lord look here!", Duane called out. "A big rattlesnake." "My god!", Uncle Grady said, "You are a lucky one today. Four or five feet over and you would have crawled right out on top of him. It's a wonder old Sport didn't get bit." By then Whit had walked up and the snake was sent to his eternal rest by a blast from a twelve gauge double barreled shotgun. It was over five feet long. They hung him up on a limb on the road by the head so all the other hunters could see and be warned, "rattle snakes are here". It was a common courtesy. This place came to be known by the clan as "Rattle Snake Head", and many a time after that, one would here, "I'll meet you at Rattle Snake Head." And always when it was mentioned, in the memory of the mind, came, "Watch out for snakes".

I go there often to meet with the spirit of the men there (they have long passed on by way of all the earth, dog and rattle snake included) and we walk together in my memory around the head and down the branch of the Rattle Snake Head. I loved these men, probably because they loved me so much. And the dog? I loved him too and I know he loved me. And his intermittent flaw? We didn't care. We understood. We were there for birds and so was Sport. I see them there and my heart is filled simultaneously with joy and grief ; joy for the great men and great times, grief that I might not have fulfilled their highest expectations. I go away refreshed with new visions and new hopes as their spirit fills me, as it always has, with righteous feelings of meaningful purpose. I knew these men you see, because I am Duane, the singing lion.

Don't Shoot

*I*t was in the afternoon after a morning hunt that my dad (Whit Broxson), my uncle (Grady Broxson) and a dear friend, Wade Bishop, started up a gentle rise toward an isolated wet weather head in an open stand of large longleaf pines and wiregrass turf. You could see clearly all around this head resting on the edge of a gently rising hill because very little oak brush grew there. We were hunting for singles as the local talk goes and the bird dogs were working the rising ridge before us as we approached the green head and the small wet weather branch that trickled down into the larger creek below. We expected to start picking up singles around this old green head and possibly below it on the thinly covered branch. I was walking in front of my dad who was a few steps behind me. Uncle Grady and Wade were off to the left. The green head was about three hundred yards above and to the left of us. We were hunting late in the quail season which extended even into March. Deer and turkey season were closed and only fine shot were allowed on the Black Water Forest Management area. It's lands extended from Cold Water Creek near Milton Florida to the Alabama state line some thirty to forty miles distant. We came here often in the spring to hunt turkey gobblers, and to take a fine turkey gobbler was something to brag about among the hunters of the area. All three of us were woodsmen of a sort, my dad, uncle and friend were accomplished expert woodsmen and had spent most of their life there. We were acutely aware of everything going on. We were scanning the area before us and carefully watching the dogs as they worked the clear area under the tall longleaf pines. Trudging through the thick wire grass with my worn out brogans and improvised spats was difficult to say the least, since we had walked all morning up and down hills like these. Suddenly as I walked along a huge turkey gobbler just stood up right in front of me, not more than ten feet away. It had squatted in the wire grass as the dogs commenced to work the area and had to flee because we were going to walk right over it. My first impulse of course was to shoot, which everyone knew I could do lightening fast and with deadly accuracy. But the presence of my father caused me to hesitate and to half turn and exclaim, "Papa Look!" As Papa looked up he instantaneously and with a sort of reverent stern inflection exclaimed, "Don't shoot! Don't shoot" To me any of my dad's commands came as if from the heart of God himself and I checked. By then the turkey had flown and was heading out across the open wire grass landscape. As Wade saw the bird fly away he raised his gun and fired and so did I, motivated as I was by his action. The bird, by then, was much too far away for fine shot from a shotgun. The bird never wavered on its course up through the tall pines and on to the other branches on the other side of the hill. Wade turned to me and exclaimed , "Why didn't you shoot it?!" To which my dad replied: "It's out of season and no one should have shot at him."

I know now as I reflect on this incident why I looked back that day. I was looking for my dad's approval because I knew it was out of season and I knew how my dad felt about upholding the law and doing what was right. My dad also knew me and knew that if he had not been there, I would have shot that bird with the lightening speed that I was known to have. In the depths of my conscious mind this little incident of on the spot teaching in a familiar place and with the most influential persons ever to enter my life has always been a guiding principle. The principle is not just don't shoot turkeys out of season and my daddy knew that. I here its profound exclamation every time I am faced with a difficult situation where I know I am heading in the wrong direction, and it helps me to check, to reach down for that connection to wise instruction from a wise woodsman whom I loved so much. I go there often, and as I look out over the landscape, the love of my father fills me, and his clear understanding of the right thing to do, gives me reason to do likewise.

To my family and friends who knew these men and to others who might read and understand, I would like to offer a suggestion. Remember these kinds of places in your life as did the Western Apache at Cibecue; Green head lying in wiregrass on hillside of longleaf pine, at this very place, because " Wisdom Sits in Places." "Wisdom Sits in Places" is a book by Dr. Keith Basso about the Western Apache Indian culture and language. I recommend that you read it.

Double Heads

*T*his place was called Double Heads because of the two heads on each side of the road. Cherry Branch head on the east side and Buck Branch head on the west side. It was here that many times the old hunting party of Broxson brothers would meet to begin a hunt. Sometimes this would entail as many as twelve vehicles or more..

Grady, Whit and Duane would meet Willie and T. J. at Grandfather Broxson's old home on the north side of the river. There, usually, Grady and Whit would leave with T. J. and Duane would leave with Willie. Later either Whit or Grady would ride with one of their other brothers, or both of them would. Grady, Whit, T. J., Duane , Willie, C. L. Williams, Earl Farrington, Billy McClellan and others, would trail the roads for buck sign up the south side of Yellow river, around Cherry Branch and More Creek and on across Boiling Creek to the bridge on Wolf Creek. Those coming from Holly; Frank, Faircloth, Walter, Hobson, Clayton and others, would trail the Line of Twelve road, the Board Pile Road, the Red Road at Weaver Tower, the Sapling Sinks Road, the Mail Route Road and most of the other roads to the south of the head of More Creek. They would then meet at a predetermined place to discuss the strategy for the first morning hunt. Often they would meet at Double Heads, but sometimes they would meet at the Black Bottom or other designated place. They would decide which buck sign found was the best for the first hunt. Each driver of a truck or vehicle would then be designated a place to go to "stand " for the first hunt. Everyone would depart and go to his designated place. After everyone had time to get into place, the person who was to release his dogs would go to the place the deer sign had been located. He would release his dogs and the dogs would slow trail the deer until the deer "jumped". The standers knew to stay in place and not move and make noise. This could sometimes take hours or sometimes minutes. There were no CB radios then but the hunters knew well what was happening. Each hunter could recognize each dog's bark and knew the barking pattern for all of the dogs when they were trailing deer. Each dog had a different sound, rhythm and pattern for barking. The barking dogs would obviously alert the hunters about the direction the deer had taken as it went to lie down that morning, usually shortly before, or right after daybreak. Where the deer lay down, would usually determine the most probable place it would leave the enclosed area. There were never enough hunters to cover every spot around the area the deer was in, but the most probable places were covered. They knew these places well and also knew, "off the cuff", the order of the probability based on where the deer "jumped". The deer knew well that the dogs were on their trail, but usually they would wait until the dogs were fairly close before leaving the area. A buck deer would usually get up and try to slip out of the area well before the dogs reached his lie. Often he would circle back behind the dogs before they "jumped" to throw them off. The hunters knew this strategy and often the hunter that released the dogs would follow them quietly, always watching for this to happen. T. J was one to do this often. Hunters could tell when the dogs were approaching the place where the deer would "jump" because the barking rhythm would gradually increase. Everyone waited for the shot to ring out from that most probable place. Many times it would as the hunters listened to the dogs "jump" and begin an all out chase of the deer. What a thrill it was to listen to this happen. You could just here the excitement in the dogs barks as they began to drive the deer. If a shot had rung out, one of two things would happen. Either the dogs would reach the place where the shot rang out and stop, or they would go on passed this point. If they stopped the chase was over. The deer was dead. If they continued, it could mean one of two things. There was one deer and the hunter had missed his shot. For our party, that also meant the deer was a buck deer. It could also mean there were more than one deer and one or more had continued on. Everyone began contemplating the next most probable place to cut off the deer. Those that needed to, moved toward the next most likely places. Some hunters remained still because they were already in one of them. Those places were well known by the hunters and they would not run up on a stander on his stand. This would continue until the deer was killed, or crossed some boundary, or went to a body of water, which could be a river, creek or bay in an attempt to lose the dogs. It was inevitable that sometimes the dogs would be lost and a dog hunt would ensue. Most hunters trained their dogs to return on the backtrack of the deer to the place the chase had begun. T. J. trained his dogs to do this. Sometimes when deer were run into the river and crossed the river, T. J.'s dogs would go home to his house across the river. Many a night Whit and Duane would wait for T. J to whistle his dogs out of a swamp somewhere, because Whit would not leave until the owner of the dog went home or the dog was found.

When the original area that a deer was in was large and the deer was a buck behind fast dogs, he would usually make one large circle and then head toward one of those safety areas mentioned above. If he was jumped in a river swamp, he could go straight into the river or run out of the swamp and out on the hillside in an attempt to lose the dogs. Of course, the hunters knew every place a deer would use to pass out of a enclosed island (flat open meadow) in a swamp, and they would stand at those places.

Usually when the deer were does, they would wait until the last minute to leave their lie. They would dodge and circle the dogs, sometimes in sight of the dogs. This gave a characteristic pattern to the running of the dogs and experienced hunters could, most of the time, tell if the dogs were running does. Of course, if the dogs ran through a stand and there was no shot, it was probably a doe and the hunter could not catch all of the dogs. If the dogs stopped at a stand and did not continue and there was no shot, the hunter had successfully stopped the dogs and the deer were does.

Sometimes when the deer jumped was a buck, it would purposefully run in on a group of does and then dodge out and watch for the dogs to pick up the track of the does which left more trail for them to follow.

The men of the William Milton Broxson family knew the land they grew up on like the back of their hand. They knew all of the deer runs and turkey roosts. It was their life. It was their love. They were the most honest, caring, law-abiding men I have ever met, and not just because they were my family. The deer woods around the old Broxson homestead, on Yellow River in Santa Rosa County Florida, with the William Milton Broxson Hunting Party, was the best place for a young boy to grow up. No drinking, no foul talk about anything, no breaking of the law, no complaining were unspoken standards they lived by. They were tough mentally and physically and they expected you to be tough. They respected and cared for each other and expected that of you also. It was an honor and a joy to have been part of this great family.

The Cow Trail

Once many years ago, the Broxson party had found where a big buck deer crossed the road down in the Crain Islands, as the open flat next to Yellow River was called at this point. T. J. Broxson, Whit Broxson's youngest brother was going to put his dog on the trail of the deer. All of the men of the party discussed where they were going to stand to cut the deer off. The deer could cut back into the river or he could go out through the bay-gall to the hill side. Whit, Grady, Duane and L. L. McCombes (the local barber), thought the deer would go out on the hillside because it was late in the day. Whit and Grady stationed themselves at the gap where the road entered the swamp and along the road between there and the Juniper head. L. L. and Duane went past Juniper Head to the Cow Trail, as it was called, to stand for the deer. L. L. placed himself down at the swamp where the trail left the swamp. Duane, giving L. L. plenty of room, moved down the road about one hundred yards. Willie, Frank, Walter, Faircloth, and Hobson stayed inside the islands along the inner road to cut him off from the river.

Uncle T. J.'s dog (Bell) was a spayed blue tick female that didn't bark much but was fast as lightening and did not allow a deer, even a seasoned buck, any running room. Duane listened as Bell began to trail the deer. He listened carefully and intently because Bell did not bark much and one had to pay close attention. He heard her when she

DUANE BROXSON. THE TEACHER

jumped the old buck just inside the flat next to the bay-gall. Boy did she push him! She made one small circle in the flat and started for the hill. She never faltered, her barks sparse and far between, but Duane knew this dog, and knew she was pushing him fast out of the swamp. She was probably almost running in sight of him. Duane had seen Bell running in sight of many deer, mostly does. On she pushed him right toward the Cow trail. Duane knew he was due to come out any second. L. L. was right in place, he listened for him to shoot. L. L. did not shoot. After a moment Duane heard the crackling of a bush down by the swamp. As he turned to look down that way, he saw him! A huge buck with an eight point rack at least, slipping along parallel to the swamp in Duane's direction. He had slipped out past L. L. and he did not see him! On past Duane's position on the road he went and Duane moved quickly but carefully up the road to another position. The deer was about sixty yards ahead of Duane as it turned up the hill to cross the road. Duane started to shoot at him on the hillside, but it was too thick with scrub to get a good shot through. Duane was ready as he crossed the road about sixty yards in front of him. Duane raised his old bolt action twelve gage and let him have a load of number one buck shot as he left the road on the other side. The deer stopped short in a breaking lunge but did not fall. Duane knew he had hit him. He tucked his tail and turned, moving across the hill on the other side of the road, right toward Duane. Duane knew his old gun's action did not work consistently. It sometime jammed. Most of the time it jammed when it was worked slowly. Duane intentionally (he did not get overly excited) worked the action quickly with force, and you guessed it, it jammed. It turned the shell sideways to the chamber and jammed it into the receiver. Duane tried frantically to remove the jammed shell but it would not budge. The deer passed right in front of Duane about forty steps away struggling at a fast walk, it's tail tucked and its head down, a sure sign of injury. It would have been an easy shot. Old bell came out into the road about that time and the deer turned up the hill and struggled off at a run. Duane knew the deer had been his, but this is life and it got away. Duane knew that his uncles would tease him

Short Stories

about being so excited and jamming the gun, but this had not happened. He told them the truth, but felt that they did not believe him.

Duane was always calm in a situation that required immediate action, he never got so excited he couldn't think clearly. This characteristic would save his life many years later, as his aircraft pitched violently upward from the runway in a sure death situation.

The deer went quickly across the hill and down into the mouth of Long branch and into Boiling Creek. It was almost nightfall. The dogs (more dogs had been placed on the track) were heard baying at night fall on the bank of the creek. Duane was just a boy so he could not demand that a search be made for the deer along the creek that night. It was a difficult swamp with several branches running into it at this point. Duane always believed that had it been daytime , the deer would have been recovered and the loss amended. It was said that a large deer was found dead along this creek several weeks later. This was one of Duane's most regretful moments other than the regretful loss of a woman's love (not his divorced wife) many, many years after that. May God bless his soul.

Whit and Jim and More Creek Head

*O*nce my uncle Jim Harter accompanied my dad, Whit Broxson, hunting around the old Broxson home place. The dogs jumped several deer and ran them out on the hill toward the heads of the branches. Whit and Jim cut off the dogs here at the head of More Creek and Whit killed two deer in the same place.

My dad cautioned Jim about entering the military service because of the war but Jim was determined to join the fighting forces for his country. He later joined the navy and sacrificed his life for his country off the coast of Salerno Italy. My mother's family were devastated. My grandmother never gave up hope of seeing her youngest son again.

The great love this family had for one another still touches my heart today. If the majority of our young people today could grow up experiencing this kind of love , we wouldn't need to worry about drugs and vice overcoming the American people. My grandmothers love for her son motivated me to write the poem "Uncle Jim" in his and her honor. I loved them and they loved me. What more can anyone say?

Cherry Branch Head

It was on this branch that Whit Broxson killed his first deer as a boy. He had run on foot from the mouth of Boiling Creek out to this branch head to cut off the deer and the dog that was running it. He shot it with an old Sharps rifle from a distance and hit it. Uncle Dick Broxson, Whit and others trailed the deer until they found him.

Whit Broxson was very good with a rifle or shotgun. He was the best shot in the party of Broxson brothers. His shots were always in the kill area and one shot was all that was usually needed. His brother T. J. was called "Sure Shot" but he was not as good as Whit either at shooting deer or quail. He acquired that title because he had killed so many deer and seemed to always be in the right place to get a deer, but his shots were never as clean or as few as Whit. Whit was deadly. A buck deer had better not pass within shotgun or rifle range of Whit or he never left the area. T. J. also hunted every day of a deer season whereas Whit could only hunt a few days each season. T. J. had a storage shed at home that was about twelve feet by fourteen feet. The entire outside walls were covered with deer horns from the deer he had killed and those were not all of them. Duane Broxson and Whit Broxson were about equals at shooting quail on the wing. Much better than T. J or Grady. They were experts and seldom missed. Duane was quicker than Whit, T. J or Grady on wing shots at quail. Grady was a fair shot but nothing close to Whit or Duane.

DUANE BROXSON. THE TEACHER

Grady, Whit, T. J and Duane hunted many a season for quail and tur-keys on Yellow River and in the Blackwater State Forest after the deer season was over. These were great days with great men for Duane. There was never any misunderstanding or argument. Each one would do anything for the others. . They pressed hard every moment as if it was the work they were called to do. Stopping a grueling hunt (they always walked and never used vehicles or horses to hunt quail) to eat a lunch of sardines, caned beans and bread, was for Duane, "Oh Wil-derness were Paradise enow!" Of course you know he would't trade this for the real meaning of this quote from the Rubaiyat of Omar Kkhayyam!

Walter and the Chain Saw

I was a teacher at Munson High School in Santa Rosa County Florida for sixteen years, teaching physics, chemistry, biology and seventh and eighth grade science. I had the opportunity to see children grow and mature, intellectually, physically and emotionally. I was a teacher of students first and then a teacher of science. This allowed me to generate a lot of rapport and respect among students. They trusted me and confided in me often. I was a carpenter when young and knew most of the housing construction skills. I was a civil aviation pilot and taught aviation ground school. I had extensive training in Medical Technology before beginning a teaching career. Students respected me for this and knew that I knew and understood the science I was teaching.

Some political unrest had arisen in the community over the administration of the school and the choice of personnel. So much so that a dissatisfied political faction enticed a student to burn the old school down. It was a great loss. It was constructed in nineteen twenty seven and was a valuable and cherished piece of history in the community. It's loss almost caused the closure of the school but community and elected officials vowed to rebuild the school. While construction was being conducted, we taught in the gymnasium. The county school work crew partitioned the gymnasium into classrooms. The working conditions were very difficult. The partitions were only eight feet

DUANE BROXSON. THE TEACHER

high with no ceiling. A continuous roar of noise filled the gymnasium during school session and gnats were so bad one could hardly open one's mouth without eating a few. Huge fans were stationed at the doorways to attempt to cool the place down in the summer and to help blow away the gnats. The teacher's lounge and work room was located in the back of the gymnasium in an old book room full of moisture and mildew. Everyone got sinus infections, including the principal, who had to be admitted to the local hospital. We had a great faculty and staff. Most were good country folks that just buckled down and did what they had to do and made teaching through these years successful.

I was sitting in the musty, mildewed teacher's lounge one afternoon working on assignments, when I saw one of our students running as hard as he could up the hall toward me. He ran through the door and stopped in front of me gasping for breath. "Mr. gasp, gasp, Mr. Broxson, gasp, You gotta----You gotta come quick! gasp, Walter's cut his throat with a chain saw!" What! I said, "Walter's cut his *throat* with a *chain* saw!? Yes, Yes! He said, You gotta come quick!! I jumped up and followed him at a run down the hall. When I passed the room where coach West was teaching, I yelled, "Coach! Come quick! An emergency!!" He left his room at a run and caught up with us outside. Running beside us, he hollered, "What's happened!?" "Walter's cut his throat with a chain saw!" I yelled. As we ran on toward the trees beyond the agricultural plot behind the school, we met several students running hard toward us, "Walter's cut his head off with a chain saw!" One of the boys yelled, intentionally increasing the drama of the episode. My mind was racing, trying to anticipate my actions when I reached him. All three of us were running as hard as we could to reach him. We could see the students gathered around a large oak tree. As we came closer, we could see Walter sitting, with his back leaning against the tree with his head down. The students (some of them were girls) were crying and wailing around him. I began to slow down as I approached Walter. I could see him clearly now and I could

Short Stories

not see any blood on his shirt below his neck or on his chest. My tension eased a little. As I drew up to Walter, coach West began consoling the students who were weeping and crying, "Walter's dying! Walter's dying!" Walter was passed out with his head down and his chin on his chest. I raised his head and there on his throat was a large slash from one side of his throat to the other, but there wasn't much blood and no visible pulse of blood or flow could be seen. I looked more closely and realized that the cut was only skin deep. It had cut only the skin and no deeper! Walter had just passed out from the fright and shock! The students around were still weeping and crying, "Walter's dying! Oh Walter's dying! I yelled at them, "Walter's not dying! He's just passed out! Walter's ok! Walter's ok! I raised Walter's head up and slapped him lightly on the face. He came to momentarily and looked at me, but then he let out a moaning cry and passed out again! The students began crying again, "Walter's dying, Walter's dying! I yelled at them to get hold of themselves, that Walter was ok. I asked someone to call 911 for an ambulance. I continued to shake and slap Walter until he awakened and began to put some pressure on a cloth over the wound. It was a large but superficial cut. Walter eventually stabilized and the children calmed down. We stayed with him until the ambulance came to pick him up.

What an experience that had been. A frightening and gruesome fear had been relieved and all was well! I have often reflected on this incident. Wesley (the boy who came for me) had run by the Principal's office, by the coach's open door, all the way down the long hallway to reach me. I was moved by this. I loved those kids.

The Battle

*N*ow and then a blinding flash of light sends its message to an anxious war party which is stationed high above the rocky cliffs. Some careless soldier moving for a better position has let the rays of the sun strike the brightly polished magazine of his well kept Winchester.

A stern face glances about over the enemy below. Small Bear enumerates his enemy. His well trained eye scans the rocks and cliffs which rise above the canyon floor.

Captain Martin holds his position behind a high bolder in front of his small scouting party of men and prays for deliverance as he faces the slowly enclosing danger. The small band of soldiers determine strategy for the arising battle.

The sun beats down upon the desert floor and sends steaming gushes of hot air bellowing above the summits of the mountains beyond. The great luminous ball rises higher and higher in the sky as it pours down its rays upon the dried out land.

Soon, as the sun reaches its climax, enemy will meet enemy. The fight will have begun. The sands of the desert will record the conflict of man against man. The driving force of a poison dipped arrow will tear the chest of a hard fighting soldier. The painted skin of a sun hardened brave will spatter with blood as a bullet rips through his body. Arrow will follow arrow. Shot will follow shot till the sun lowers its rays below the shadowy horizon, and the cool mountain air descends to the sands of the canyon. Slowly, as the night advances, the crimson moon will begin its curving arc across the sky. Then, silence, still silence, silence that makes the dead rest peacefully in honor of battle, and the living weep in sorrow.

The Silent Valley

*S*oft golden beams of light slowly penetrate the dark forest. Tall trees stand as towering giants in the silent valley where sparkling spring water trickles over the rocks from the hills above. Blades of grass weep with small droplets of dew, as the sun sends its rays to the meadow below. The whispering breeze of the cool morning air echos sounds of the awaking forest. A young buck deer slips silently to the flowing stream and stands motionless sniffing the resh morning air. Suddenly he gives a bolting leap as an arrow pierces the dark brown hair of his smooth shoulder. The young deer falls gasping for breath! The rippling water is stained with blood that gushes from the wound. The forest is awakened with a cry of wrath! The sound goes out, a frightening sound. The Jay birds scream the cry of danger! A startling cry that came too late.

A day has come. A life is taken. The sun settles beneath the rising hills of the shaded valley. A young doe looks anxiously out over the crimson meadow and smells the heat of fresh spilled blood. She turns, pauses and then slips silently into the awaiting night. All is quiet in the silent valley.

Pretty Flower by the Field Fence Line

*T*here was potential in the young flower growing by the fence down first base line. No one would ever know it though just to look at it. It was a polyploid. The only one of its kind on earth at that time. What potential it possessed no one could really know, but different it was, for sure. It could have come this way through the grass sprigs brought in to replenish the infield, or by bird on the fence, as many a row of sweet fruit have come. Who knows how it got there, but it was surely by chance, pretty little flower growing by the field fence line.

It was the last and deciding game of the World Series at Grant Stadium that day. When Harvey came to bat in the ninth inning, two men were out and three runners were on base. The score stood two to three. As he approached the plate, the umpire, who had met Harvey at the university and was his friend, casually commented, "Did you know Harvey, I learned today that this is the age of the bacteria! Could you have ever believed that"? To which Harvey replied, "Well, yes - we've been knowing this for some time now. The umpire replied, "Is that a fact"! I also heard that life here on Earth is just an insignificant blip in all of the universe. And what is more amazing, that man is just an even smaller blip of the chance unfolding of life on the Earth! To which Harvey replied, "Well, yes - We've also known this for some time" (interrupted by cries from the fans: "Harvey! Harvey! - Harvey! Harvey!) "Listen Jimmy, I'll talk to you about this later. It is really fascinating but my team is down now by three to two and what I really need to know is what kind of stuff this pitcher has." To which the umpire quickly replied, "I'm sorry Harvey. You know better than that! That's against the rules of baseball!" "Oh, I was just kidding you ump! I'm watching for that change up curve after that side arm inside fastball!" Harvey replied.

The stadium had been built with a short right field fence with Harvey in mind. Harvey was a strong and powerful hitter who could hit to any field. His eye was good and his swing was smooth and powerful. He pulled the ball well, as his right field home run record would reveal. He thought like a pitcher, for he too had begun baseball as a pitcher. Harvey took the first pitch right down the middle for a strike, but he got a good look at the ball. The next pitch, however, was an overhand fastball, brushing him back from the plate. Harvey was ready now. He knew when the pitcher's arm came over, by the light between his arm and head, that the overhand, change up outside curve was coming. His powerful arms came around. He was out in front, topping but blasting the ball foul to the fence down right field line. He had missed his pitch! The crowd roared!, "Harvey! Harvey!, Harvey! Harvey!" Harvey thought quickly. "The last time he did that, he came back with another inside fastball and then the inside screwball for a strike. I'll be ready for that brush back pitch". The pitcher delivered the next pitch with all of his might and soul. A powerful, overhand, inside, slider fastball, brushing Harvey back at the plate. The pitcher was a young man, lean and powerful. He was more or less self taught. He had learned most of his pitching from his father, though he had never tried to play organized ball in school. He had just walked on one of the minor league teams. He thought about what his father had taught him and what he had learned from experience. He contemplated what the batter might be thinking. He knew the last time he had thrown the inside screwball and got the batter out on a called strike, but this guy was smarter than that. He waved off the first sign from the catcher. Now he had his sign. Stretching from the full windup, Joshua reached back with all of his might and strength. Harvey was ready. He knew the inside screwball was coming. Joshua delivered the pitch. A screaming ninety mile per hour, side arm but sinking screwball. Harvey never flinched back. He swung with all of his might! The bat was dead on the pitch that he knew was going to straighten at the last moment. The pitch straightened. The bat streaked toward the ball accelerated with all of Harvey's strength! For the first time in years the catcher's eye blinked for less than an instant. The crowd roared! The fans jumped to their feet! The players ran out onto the field in wild jubilation! "Joshua! Joshua!" One of the players cried. "How do you do it!? How do you do it!?" "Oh it just comes natural". Joshua replied.

Pretty flower by the field fence line,
What more but chance could place you there,
To sprout a tid-bit blip in space and time,
But who would know, or who could care?

Pretty, pretty flower on the field fence line,
Withered, broken, lying in my hand,
If I could know your all in all,
And why your fate by Harvey's ball,
As all unfolds from now to flaming end of earthly time,
I should see that natural, is what is.

The Last Spin[26]

had grown much older now, I must have been in my nineties. I was still in good health and alert mentally. I decided to go over to General Clay McCutchen's private field and see if he would let me solo my old J3 cub again. He had purchased my old plane and kept it in his hanger at the field. With some reluctance, he agreed to check me out to see if I could possibly do this. Well I surprised him. My old touch came back from all those years of flying this plane and I could fly it as good if not better than he. He decided to let me take it out solo. I left his field at Harold, Florida and headed out west north west toward the old farm fields north of Allentown just west of the Whiting Field controlled air space. I began to do aerobatics over the fields as I had done years ago. I did loops, hammerhead turns, chandelles, Immlemans, and steep turns. I was having a ball. Then I decided to do one of my favorite maneuvers, the vertical spin. It was a joy to do in an old J3. I climbed to about three thousand feet and started to execute the maneuver. I pulled the power back to idle and maintained altitude with increasing back pressure on the old joy stick. When the airspeed indicator had passed by the twenty mark, the old door flopped up, the J3's own unique stall indicator. As the door flopped up, the plane started to drop. I kept the old joy stick crammed back into my belly and quickly popped the left rudder pedal to the floor and held it there.

---

[26] This writing is part of a larger writing, "The Flowers of Spring"

Short Stories

The old J3 quickly rolled left, pitched nose down and began to spin around its vertical axis. I could see the fields I loved spinning below me and I just let it turn and tighten up a bit. I saw the upper wing when it separated from the fuselage and flew back over the tail section. The plane pitched more violently down and accelerated greatly toward the ground. I could see the cotton field turning wildly below me getting ever larger and larger. In the instant I saw the blur of the white cotton on the stalks I awakened from my dream.......And found myself sitting in the Volkswagen, in front of my old home, kissing Jerrie Lee.

Gopher Sense

I have always believed that animals, in general, have more intelligence and insight than scientists in their formal writings gave them. This view did not come from any analytical process on my part but from observations of animals in their own environments and niches. From the time I was a small boy until college age, I hunted and fished with my dad and uncles continuously. We hunted on the lands of North West Florida, predominantly on Balckwater State Forest and Eglin Air Force Reservation. Deer hounds and the English Setters and Pointer dogs of quail hunting were like family to me and we worked extensively together as a team. I will have to tell you that I loved those animals and knew every nuance of their behavioral characteristics. Not only this kind of observation but observation of animals in their own niches in the wilderness also fascinated me. Crows (*Corvus brachyrhynchos pascuus*) were one of them. It just seemed to me that they knew a great deal about what was "going on" in the forest and they in some respects were "intuitive". When I read the article, "A Birdbrain Nevermore" By Dr. Bernd Heinrich in Natural History Magazine, I knew that my assessments were not completely anthropomorphic. I did not study in science to become a research scientist and I did not do experimental research, but I did become very familiar with all disciplines of science and gave them all much thought from a scientific and philosophical view point. I taught science in the secondary high school for thirty five years so I had plenty of opportunity to do this. I had one way conversations with Dr. Stephen Jay Gould about consciousness and the prospect of a "human like consciousness" existing or arising in other animals. I also considered human culture and social behavior to be just as much a part of "natural nature" as any other behavior exhibited by animals in nature since we are all entwined together in the evolution of life from the very beginning. Dr. Gould spoke to some of these views through his writings in "This View of Life" in Natural History Magazine. He was of the view, and rightly so, that not much could come of just "thinking" about science. One had to become engaged in the activity of research science, observing, hypothesizing, and testing, allowing your thoughts and views to be scrutinized by others. You are known by your "works" he would probably say. This brings me to the reason I wrote this short article. Well Dr. Gould, God bless you wherever you are. I know you still live in my own heart and mind. Nature has provided me with an experiment and I would like to present it here for others to review and evaluate.

I constructed a garden at the site of my new home. I say, constructed, because I had to build a chicken wire fence around it to keep rabbits and deer from destroying it. The fence wire was buried a few inches under the surface to keep the rabbits out. Shortly thereafter, I noticed a gopher tortoise (*Gopherus polyphemus*) had dug its hole at the fence line with the opening on the outside of the garden facing north east, thirty degrees east of north to be exact. It was a very small gopher and I watched it grow over a few years into a larger but still small gopher.

When I was young we hunted the gopher tortoise for food. We used a pole constructed of lengths of grape vine taken from the forest hammocks. We bound them together to make a pole over twenty five feet long. To one end we attached a metal hook. We would hook the gopher and pull him out of the hole. If you think that sounds easy then you have never "pulled" gophers. Their holes could be twenty five or more feet long and eight or more feet deep at the end. The angle varied with depth, getting steeper further down the hole.

As the years went by, the fence became exposed at the mouth of the hole, rusted and broke off. One day I noticed the gopher inside the garden changing the entrance opening so it would open into the garden. Some time later, I went over to investigate and saw where the gopher had eaten one of my bean plants at the end of the row. He had gained access to my garden through the fence. I sealed the wire hole and blocked the gopher's access. Several days I watched the mouth of the hole for activity. Activity was scant. The following Sunday morning I went out to check my garden. I noticed a mound of dirt in the pea patch. I knew immediately what it was. I was excited because I also knew what this gopher had done. It could not gain access to my garden through the fence anywhere, so it dug a new entrance. But wait! This was no ordinary incident. This gopher had dug this hole from the bottom up. Beginning from many feet down the original hole, this gopher had drastically changed the angle thirty or more degrees and dug up to achieve access to my garden. In the wild a gopher would not need to do this and I have not observed a situation where I thought this had happened. I know they change the mouth of the hole when it becomes blocked, but this hole was not blocked. It was the access to my garden that was blocked and the gopher purposefully changed the angle from below. To me, this requires some degree of insight. The gopher had to "know" that this hole would open in the garden before he started digging it or he wouldn't have. Granted, it could be very minimal but insight never the less. What do you think?

For many years now, I have pondered over an explanation that would bridge the gap between our complex consciousness and self awareness and that of other animals. By embracing the principle of evolution one can gain insight into this difficulty. Our own consciousness, self awareness, intent and purpose has evolved over millions of years beginning with the simplest heterotrophs. We did not become self aware suddenly one day, but evolved it through a long process, beginning with the simplest responses to our environment, and our own body monitoring mechanisms, and the feedback we received from those responses. Motion and the ability to recognize motion, I believe, is the key to the kind of intuitive self awareness and consciousness we possess. It is my view that even some of the simplest heterotrophs have an "awareness" of self in its own environment as it interacts with it in its particular niche. This, I believe, is the key, the conditions of its particular environmental niche. What kind of awareness does an aunt have of itself and its environmental niche? No one knows because we cannot live as it does under the conditions of its environmental niche. As it interacts in specific ways to the experiences in its environment and its own bodily functions, it receives feedback as it makes responses. It is this feedback that allows a perception of self however rudimentary. Of course, that perception is not "readable" in our literal complex conscious system. It is "readable" only in the context of the aunt's experiences and its own programmed neurons. Magnify these kinds of experiences from generation to generation though the millions of years of our own existence through the forms we have taken, and we can see a fundamental process that has unfolded in every advanced heterotroph that has led some (not necessarily, as Gould would indicate) to a higher awareness, a higher order consciousness. Competition with one another and motion, I believe, has fired this higher order consciousness in some animals including ourselves. Look at the kind of consciousness some of the graizers have and compare it with the consciousness of some of the carnivores and omnivores including ourselves, where competition was keener and greater. Looking back, I believe that many animals had the same "potential" to reach our level of consciousness, obviously we did. We are what we are today, because of our experiences of yesterday. Experience is also a grand player. What other characteristics in another lineage of life, in this world or in another world, that being subjected to sustaining experiences, could result in another consciousness and self awareness resembling ourselves, that could be called by itself, a coincidental after thought of nature?

A Fish To Keep

*O*nce my nephew (Howie Gillis) and myself decided to go fishing in some small lakes in the old Crain Islands in Eglin Air Force Base. We had to cross this bridge on Boiling Creek to get there. We stopped momentarily to look around as we almost always do. While we were there I began to fish around some grass near the boat landing. I caught a small bream. I told Howie that I was not going to release him because we might not catch anything and I didn't want to go home empty handed. I took a fine nylon line and threaded it through the gill in a loop. I threw the fish back into the water and hooked the end of the line on a bush nearby. We went on to the other fishing site and guess what? Yes, you guessed it, we didn't catch any fish. When we started back home and came to the bridge, we stopped to get my fish to take home. When I pulled the line up out of the water, I didn't have a fish. I had a Cotton Mouth Moccasin snake on the end of the line. I pulled him up on the bank, got a stick and knocked him in the head. In the meantime, the fish had come out of his mouth as I pulled him around to strike him. I washed the fish off, took him home and ate him with some other fish we had. I would have released him had I caught a few fish at the other site. Now I know you think this is ridiculous, but we Broxson's know better. No fish taste better to us than a crisply fried small bream. They are ten times better than a six pound bass, and sometimes they are just as much fun to catch.

Boiling Creek Bridge

*M*y dad and I have sculled up boiling creek many times. I personally have sculled from the mouth of Boiling Creek, to this bridge without stopping for any length of time, maybe for a coke, or to get a bait untangled. I remember once Jimmy Wolfe and I made this trip. Jimmy could not handle the boat well enough, so I let him fish. I enjoyed sculling and watching someone fish as much as fishing myself. Just as we left the landing at the mouth, Jimmy sighted a Cotton Mouth Moccasin snake in an old hollow tree just above the water line. I eased the boat up to the tree and he hit the snake in the head with the oar. He lifted the snake up on the end of his oar and said he would like to keep it. He was interested in studying Herpetology. I said, "Ok, Just put him in the well." We were in one of Uncle Dick's old boats from Nicholas Creek and it had a water well in the center. I lifted the lid and he threw him in. I sculled him on up this creek. He caught several bass and we put them in the well. Sometime a little after noon, we reached the landing at the bridge. The boat had been landed bow first by myself, but at the time, I was in the bow and Jimmy was in the stern doing something. I raised the lid to the well to look at the fish, and when I did I saw the snake swirl toward the opening! It was alive! I slammed the lid back down on the well and said to Jimmy, "Jimmy! Jimmy! This snake is alive in here. It's a wonder we didn't get bit. When I lift the lid off, you take the oar and hit the snake as it comes out." Well, when I lifted the lid the snake came out, and I mean fast! Jimmy missed him as he came out of the well and he headed toward Jimmy now standing on the stern of the boat out in the water. Bam! Bam! Jimmy punched with the oar as the snake slithered quickly toward him on the stern. Bam! In a last desperate blow Jimmy struck the snake. I don't know what Jimmy would have done had he missed him that last time. I don't think Jimmy knew either!

Sometimes my father and I would go on up the creek from the bridge. We would go up to the mouth of Little Boiling and stop and have a coke and some crackers. In the old days, if we launched at this bridge and went up, we would go passed the mouth of Little Boiling to the Mouth of Indigo Creek. These trips were always a lesson in will. My dad would never tire sculling the boat. Even in the long straight runs, which are the most difficult, he would never complain. I learned to do this also. I really prided myself in this because I could do what my daddy could do. I learned not to complain when things got tough. For my father's family, to complain was a sign of weakness. I never knew then what being with this man would mean to me in the future. It would sustain me in my darkest hour and lift my soul to the heights of meaningfulness, peace and happiness. I wrote the piece, "It Was More Than Fishing", in honor of my dad. God bless you dad! Not many people knew it but he was a "Great" man. Far greater than any preacher I ever knew.

Small Fish Grand Place

*S*ome of the best memories I have of my last two sons, Joshua and Daniel, occurred here at this site. (Atwell Pond, in Eglin Reservation as viewed on Google Earth) We would come here with our fishing gear and catch the small bream that were found around the bank and at the old spillway. The boys really got a kick out of catching these small fish. They may as well have been six pound bass. They knew that these fish fried up better than six pound bass. Sometimes you could catch a bunch of them just as fast as you could bait your hook. That was the key. No boredom here. Well, sometimes.

I loved these boys. They were great kids. When I say great, I am not just boasting because they are my kids. Both of them were respected and admired by the people that knew them. They were respectful and courteous to others especially their elders. They greeted people properly and behaved in the most respectful manner. Both of them were Florida Merit Scholars. Joshua graduated from UWF Magna Cum Laude and Daniel Graduated from UCF Summa Cum Laude. Joshua at this time is a graduate student of history at UWF. Daniel is a civil engineer at Baskervill and Donovan in Pensacola.

In my childhood, I was given so many roots it was difficult for me to fly, but I did. Literally, I did. One of my goals in life was to learn to fly. I loved aviation. I would like to think I gave these boys wings, more so than roots. It was painful for me to do this but the modern world almost demands wings in order to be really successful. I catch myself looking back more so than forward these days. I know they won't forget this place, but there could have been so many, many more places. I regret this somewhat but I know in the end they will enjoy their flying. God bless you sons, I love you to the depths of my being.

A Moment to Remember

*A*s a boy I was always fascinated with flight. I was just a child when World War Two began. I would watch the news reels at the theater with my parents. Sometimes they would show the fighter planes strafing or dog fighting and I knew even then I wanted to fly one for my country and home town. Patriotism was exceptionally strong during this time.

Many years passed after the war was over and being from a humble carpenter's family made any kind of flying for me seem impossible. Oh, I built model airplanes, even though no one in my family knew anything about them, and I visited the airport often. I would ride my bicycle out to the airport and watch the Navy pilots practice touch and go landings with the old SNJ. I was too bashful to ask anyone for a ride and to impose oneself on someone was an unspoken sin in our family. Mac McKenney, a Navy Chief airplane and power plant mechanic finally taught me how to build model airplanes that would fly and became one of my best friends. He was the greatest with airplanes and engines and was an easy going, quiet man like my dad. He was also the best with fabric and tubular steel. His model airplanes were beyond belief. I was at the airport one afternoon, standing in the background as usual, just wishing I could fly in one of those planes, when Mac walked up and asked if I would like to go for a ride. Boy! I will never forget that moment. "Oh yes!" I said. I would love to go! We embarked in an old J3 Cub and flew all over the bays and rivers around Milton Florida. I was absolutely exhilarated and I knew right then I was going to fly one day.

I talked to Mac a lot about flying as I grew older and he suggested I go to Junior College and then enter the Naval Cadet program offered by the Navy back then. Well, I did attend Junior College at Pensacola Florida but after I graduated I discovered I could not meet the physical requirements for the program because of my teeth. I had become so interested in learning in the college atmosphere that this was not a big let down for me. I transferred to a college in Alabama and continued my studies of science graduating with a B.S. in Medical Technology. I began working and married soon after that. I still had an interest in aviation but with all of the responsibility of marriage and children I could not afford it. We had two children, David and Janine, and were outgoing and well liked by everyone. My wife was too anxious for the good life, however, and traded me in for a more advanced model. Some good usually comes out of every bad situation. This gave me the opportunity to pursue my desire to fly.

I frequented a local tavern where I socialized and played pool. Roger Long, one of the bartenders, was a flight instructor at the local airport. He talked me into taking flying lessons and became my flight instructor. I already knew a lot about airplanes and flying because I had , from my youth, read every thing I could about aviation. I progressed rapidly and soloed with under eight hours of instruction. Roger was not one to require a rigid protocol, but he would remind me quite often about things that I would omit or forget in my excitement. I remember quite well one incident and his comment about it. "You will forget that one day and you will never forget it again." Roger was a great guy and a fearless pilot. We did all kinds of "stuff" and I enjoyed every minute of it.

Shortly after my solo flight, I couldn't have had more than ten hours of flight time, I was doing touch and go landings at the old Peter Prince Airfield in the Cessna 150 trainer plane. As I entered the down wind leg, I noticed an airplane in the pattern in an extended down wind leg. He was making an airliner approach. I could have easily cut in front of him on my base leg but knew this was inappropriate, so I extended my down wind and waited for him to make his turn to the base leg. By the time he turned to final, I was quite some distance down wind and waited for him to pass on final before I turned into the base leg. I lined up on final and watched him approach as I closed some of the excess distance. Just as he was about to cross the end of the runway, his airplane banked sharply to the right and pitched up. He corrected quickly but just made it back to the runway where he hit with a little drift and jerked around sharply. By then I had trimmed my aircraft for forty degrees of flaps and could tell I had the numbers zeroed in. I wondered what had caused his aircraft to act so erratically and thought it must have been an updraft from part of an old pit right at the end of the runway. In any case, I was alert and watching for any trouble. I was amazed at how stable my aircraft was approaching. It was trimmed perfectly and was almost flying itself. The closer I came to the end of the runway, the more excited I became about how perfectly my approach was going. I passed over the old pit alert for any disturbance but none came. Down I came, and flared just off the end of the runway. I touched down right on the numbers as smooth as silk. Boy! Was I excited about my almost perfect landing! I advanced the throttle to full power and watched as my airspeed indicator approached rotation speed. I rotated, and when I did the nose of that Cessna pitched almost straight up I thought. I forced the yoke forward with all of my might, but there was heavy force against the yoke, it was still pitched up. I watched the airspeed collapse passed the indicated stall speed. My heart was pounding and my mind was racing . I knew if I didn't correct this quickly I was a dead man. In the split seconds that unfolded, I did not panic, I struggled for control, and then at the last possible moment, out of the corner of my eye, I caught a glimpse of those barn doors hanging down. "Flaps!" I screamed at myself. Instantaneously I began taking out flaps. "Not all at once!" My mind yelled at itself. I took out 15 degrees. The control pressure eased and the nose pitched over as if I were cresting the top of an ocean wave. In all of this I had managed to maintained directional control. The plane began to respond and I gained full control again. I took out 15 more degrees of flaps, readjusted the trim, and tried to keep from settling. That's when I noticed the power lines at the end of the runway. "Oh my God!" "Will I clear them" I thought. In my mind I lifted my feet as I went over them. I cleared them but not by much. Yes, You have guessed it. That's what he said. "One day you will forget those flaps and you will never forget them again." I haven't because I learned about flying from that.

I went on to finish my pilot training and eventually became an advanced ground school instructor. I bought an old J3 Cub just like the one Mac Mckinney took me flying in that day. I had a J3 club that allowed members to get flying time in this great old airplane. I checked out everyone in the airplane when they joined and had the privilege of flying with several Navy Cadets and Navy pilots. One of the first female Navy flight students at NAS Whiting Field was a member of my club.

Learning to fly was one of the greatest thrills of my life. Of all the things I have ever accomplished this fulfilled me the most. It was a childhood dream. I never flew the old SNJ, or T28 but I knew I could have, and I would have for my country, had I been called on to do so. I owe so much to Mac Mckenney, gone by way of all the earth. I loved that man.

Expositions

The Nature of Jesus

The <u>man</u> Jesus was not God and therefore became the embodiment of love. The <u>man</u> Jesus was the manifestation of pure, true love in the spirit of a man and therefore became the embodiment of God. For when Jesus said: "He that hath seen me hath seen the Father", He was not referring to His physical body which he knew would see death, but rather His spiritual essence which was the embodiment of God. This is what John meant, when speaking about God in terms of the nature of man. He said: "God is Love." And "every man that loveth is born of God". Jesus Himself said: "Destroy this Temple and in three days I will raise it up." He knew that man would kill his physical body which made him a man, which He likened to the house of worship, the Temple, which would be destroyed in fact and in principle, but could not kill the essence of His spirit, which was the nature of God. Jesus Himself said that God is a Spirit, and we should worship Him in Spirit and in Truth, when talking to the woman at the well. He told us that a spiritual rebirth, which would reorder our own physically inherited nature, was possible, even necessary to be able to embrace God which we could then call Father. Jesus said that His life and death would open the mind of man to this possibility. Jesus criticized those Jews who were incapable of loving him and told them that since they could not see and embrace the love of God which existed within him, they were not in communion with God the Father. He told them that His Spiritual nature existed even before Abraham was born, but they did not understand that. When Jews inquired of Jesus to show them the Kingdom, He told them they shouldn't look here or there, in this place or that place, to find the Kingdom, because the Kingdom was within them. When he said He was the way the truth and the life and that no one cometh unto the Father but by Him, He was not referring so much to His physical being as to the nature of God which he had revealed, and which in dwelled Him. In this sense, we might paraphrase that saying as: Love is the way the truth and the life, no one cometh unto the Father but by love. Hence the necessity of the rebirth of our old nature.

So, to me, it is senseless for us to argue over this doctrine or that doctrine and bring divisions among ourselves, but to seek that renewal, that rebirth, in our own lives that will allow us to love any man, regardless of his credentials, and which will allow them to see God in us through the unconditional love we give to them. After all, that is what He gave to us.

A Comment on Jerusalem

7. "Are you greater than our Ancestor Jacob?"

"People soon become thirsty again after drinking this water."

Most of humanity stands in reverent awe of Jerusalem. But it is not Jerusalem the place that holds what we need to find. It is the spirit of the suffering souls of humanity that have cried out to enlighten us amid a Holy Land of war and hatred that has made it sacred.

"Is our worship spiritual and real"?

Jerusalem, through the ages, is a view of the struggles of humanity with itself, the dastardly and the sublime. Pray that the love of G-d and the love of our brothers will become a perpetual spring within us and Jerusalem the place where it begins. What a joy that would be to see! What a blessing for humanity!

On Visions of the Heart[27]

our own personal vision of your God is real for you, because it powers the aspirations of your inner being. The aspirations of your inner being determines to a great extent the choices that you make with your free will. And yes, it can go beyond yourself and touch others and become part of their vision. This was the power of Christ, to share his inner vision with the people of his heart and the people of the world whom He loved. It was such a grand vision, such a Holy vision, that millions have really embraced it. And why? Because deep down in the inner reaches of the soul, the knowledge of its need for ones self becomes obvious, and the illuminations stand out like the sun at sunrise, as a righteous beacon of hope[28] for man.

Your empowered self is your embraced self, the one out of all the possibilities for you that experience has allowed. To a great degree, we know our embraced self through struggles, temptations, heartaches, and failures, and also from overwhelming joys and exaltations. My embraced self still stands out like that beacon of hope, reminding me each day where my real joy lies.

Promises made to others are made through your embraced self. For

---

[27]This was written to a father in an attempt to indicate that I could not break the promises that I had made to my wife and family.

[28]As a way for "Good" to over come the world.

some, to break a promise is also to break a covenant with ones self, that inner self that powers your being. For others, promises may have never been made to be kept, but for Christ they were. We cannot and should not promise to withhold our love for others. That pure and Holy love that Christ helps us to understand is the essence of that peace that passes all understanding and is not to be withheld but expressed freely to others. It transcends the selfish physical needs of our physical selves in a bond of hope, the hope of that spiritual "New Jerusalem", where no evil can enter.

The Unbroken Vow

How can not breaking a vow demonstrate to another love that your love for them is deep and genuine, good and holy? It does this by demonstrating the deep spiritual commitment that is held by the person making the vow and reveals the depth of their ability to love, for if the other love had accepted his pledge beforehand, it would also have sustained them in their time of difficulty, which always is sure to come. A person who has broken his vow to one cannot from the depths of his spirit be sure of the new vow he has made. The hope lies in the vow maker as much as the one to whom it is pledged. It is often not the person to which the vow is made that sustains the vow by their virtue or loyalty, but the vow maker's expectations of himself which is rooted in the depths of his being. To violate this would be to violate himself and all that he holds dear, to violate the very gift that he would give to the other lover.

The Magnanimous William Milton Broxson Family

*O*n Google Earth you can observe a simple bend in an old red clay road that was an old dog hunt deer run, in Eglin Air Force Proving Ground. Lessons can be learned when important things happen to people, and things happen at places. An important and moving thing happened to me at this place, that fashioned my thinking and moved my spirit. It was not asked for, it was given freely out of a caring heart from an intelligent and strong man of the woodland.

You would not believe the deep grief and emotion that my father (Whit Broxson) felt the day we stopped another party's dogs from catching a small yearling deer at this place. The small deer had been shot several times by the other party and the dogs were about to finish it off. It wobbled there bleeding and bleating about to fall. My father expressed to me the inhumanity that had taken place here that day. It was not done in anger and hatred but in utter disgust for the lack of character of the people who did this. They had not shot this deer out of need but out of the sheer thrill of killing, and they were not good shots. They had maimed the deer and not killed it outright. It was also illegal. I will always remember this. His whole family was like this. They were great people.

Sometimes really great people do not get the recognition they deserve. As beautiful as she is, I would not trade the love of my father's family for Brittany Spears, or any of the glamour of this world, because my father's family was more beautiful. Many people criticize hunters these days, but to hunt was a way of life for them. They were like the Indians who had to live off the land. They had a reverence for life and its place in the forest and on the planet that many do not understand today. They seemed to understand their relationship with other living things on the earth. They saw themselves as part of it all. They understood the giving and the taking. It was a oneness. A oneness in all aspects of life. They killed deer to sustain themselves and a way of life, just as every other animal does in his niche. We have to kill to live. This is true even if it is disguised by the atmosphere of a restaurant and someone else does the killing. Consciousness seems to reside only in animals, but even a bean seed is alive until we cook it and eat it. They did not kill just for the joy of killing. They knew that one day they would also give up their life in this grand scenario of life on planet earth.

I was in the old Broxson home one day and picked up the family bible lying on the mantel above the old fireplace. As I thumbed through it, I came to a page with some writing on it. As I began to read it, I realized it was a temperance statement given for all of his children. I cannot remember the exact words, but it made them swear that they would not partake of any alcoholic beverages or smoke cigarettes. I remember that part well. It may have had other conditions I cannot remember it in detail now. The moving thing though was the twelve signatures of his twelve children that followed the statement. Coupled with this was my knowledge of how much they loved their father and mother and how much respect they had for them. I know for a fact, that none of his children smoked cigarettes and none drank alcohol. The men would not gossip, talk about women, much less chase them, or engage openly in any immoral conversation or activity. They didn't even joke about such things. They all married and had families that they were devoted to and loved deeply. None ever divorced or left their life partner. They were willing to share anything they had when the need presented itself. They did not need to be a performer before people to obtain accolades of praise to bolster their own self esteem. They never used the likes of Satan to judge other people, or to cover for their own guilt, ignorance or misunderstanding. They never pretended to have all of the answers. They just loved each other and everyone else that would allow them to do so, and many that wouldn't. Such was the beauty of the William Milton Broxson family.

Most of the men did not attend church either that I knew of, except occasionally with their wives. I will tell you this however, I wouldn't trade these men for all of the preachers* in Northwest Florida, and there are a bunch of them. Or for the one who would brag before an audience in public about their own gross flaws in character before they were zapped by their own need for acceptance and approval disguised as a "religious" experience. These men did not tell other people how to live or try to force their views of life upon them, they just lived life to its fullest in the most righteous way I have observed since I have been alive. Mistaken are they that attempt to make the "good" man meaningless. The "good" man radiates from a heart of love, and God is Love. God bless every one of them.

I am not condemning preachers, just that I revere my family's world view more.